ROBERT C. HEERSPINK

BECOMING A FIRSTFRUITS CONGREGATION

Firstfruits, A Ministry
of the Barnabas Foundation,
Orland Park, Illinois

CRC Publications,
Grand Rapids, Michigan

RCA Foundation,
Reformed Church in America,
New York, New York

A Stewardship
Guide for
Church Leaders

Becoming A Firstfruits Congregation: A Stewardship Guide for Church Leaders, © 1996 by Firstfruits, A Ministry of the Barnabas Foundation, 15127 S. 73rd Ave., Suite G, Orland Park, IL 60462 . All rights reserved. With the exception of brief excerpts for review purposes, no part of this book may be reproduced in any manner whatsoever without written permission from the publisher. Printed in the United States of America on recycled paper. ✪ 1-708-532-3444

Library of Congress Cataloging-in-Publication Data

Heerspink, Robert C., 1953-
    Becoming a firstfruits congregation: a stewardship guide for
church leaders / Robert C. Heerspink.
        p. cm.
    Includes bibliographical references.
    ISBN 1-56212-208-8
    1. Stewardship, Christian.   I. Title.
BV772.H44   1996
254.8—dc20   96-32890
                                                                          CIP

10 9 8 7 6 5 4 3 2 1

To
my wife, Edie
and my children, Eric, Joel, and Amy
whose encouragement makes possible my stewardship of the gospel

CONTENTS

ON THE MENTION OF MONEY

W hen I entered the pastorate as a young minister just out of semi-nary, there was one topic that intimidated me. It wasn't biblical au-thority. It wasn't abortion. It wasn't sex. It was money. I was afraid to talk about money. And my congregation encouraged my fear. The message came through loud and clear in my first pastorate: "We aren't very affluent around here. So if there isn't much mon-ey for ministry, it's not our fault. Our giving is as good as it's going to get."

I bought into that deception. So I preached on the Lord's Prayer. I walked the congregation through the book of Amos. I tackled the book of Revelation. But of money and financial stewardship, I had little to say. Talk of money was confined to the yearly "Woe is us, we are undone" speech, which I delivered each fall. In effect I said, "We are behind in our church budget, but if we all do our share, we hope to be in the black by year's end."

I confess, I copped out.

I was in the pastorate for ten years before I began to discover even the rudimentary truths about financial stewardship and the role the church plays in teaching and encouraging solid financial stewardship in the con-gregation.

My conversion to serious stewardship began with an invitation from a Christian organization called the Barnabas Foundation, which was de-veloping educational material on financial stewardship entitled *Firstfruits*. The director of Barnabas asked me to field-test the program. I agreed. In the process I educated not only my congregation but myself as well. My journey to stewardship was under way.

COMPARING NOTES

Stewardship is popularly defined as a concern for time, talents, treasure, and trees. That's a comprehensive list. Unfortunately, in a study of this size we will have little time to discuss the exercise of spiritual gifts (time and talents) or ecological issues (trees). We will focus on treasure—financial stewardship. How do we as church leaders encourage kingdom citizens to demonstrate their faith through their finances? More specifically, how do we cultivate in our congregations a spirit of grateful giving as one expression of a lifestyle of stewardship?

God has always sought such an ongoing, thankful response. When their Provider blessed the Israelites with the harvest, they were to give back the best of the firstfruits of their crop by bringing it to the house of the Lord (Ex. 23:16, 19). A share of these firstfruits were given to God as a burnt offering. The rest were apportioned to the priests who served in the temple (Num. 18:12). In this way the people celebrated the Lord's rich blessings to them and provided the means to maintain a priesthood that was dedicated to serve God full-time on their behalf. This concept of God's people returning, with thanks, the first and the best of God's gifts to us, gave rise to the title of this book.

As a pastor I write for a familiar audience: fellow pastors and those serving on church boards. Through the years I have come to appreciate these faithful deacons, elders, and ministers of the Word. They care deeply about the people they serve. They invest untold hours doing their best for Christ's church. But often they are at a loss when it comes to leading their congregations in money matters. I hope that this material will help church leaders avoid the mistakes I made. This book contains many insights I've gained over the past years as I have worked with the Barnabas Foundation and with stewardship committees in my congregation.

SETTING OUR COURSE

Chapters 1-6 will expose some of the myths surrounding congregational stewardship and explore its biblical framework. The goal is to come to a clarified understanding of stewardship so that we are talking the same language. How can we teach it to others if we don't have a biblical understanding of it ourselves? We will then explore how we can apply that biblical understanding from the pulpit, investigating that intimidating discourse called a "stewardship sermon." How can we preach stewardship with integrity and conviction? Appendix A includes sermon material on a series of passages, which may be particularly useful to pastors but will also provide a resource for others who teach or speak on stewardship issues.

Chapters 7-11 will explore some concrete changes we can make in our congregational lives that will encourage a stewardship mentality in our churches. This material will be helpful to elders, deacons, and members of stewardship committees as they enable their congregations to become firstfruits congregations.

The format of this study allows for use in a group setting as well as individually. A council, consistory, or deacons' board can deal with this material in as few as two sessions, studying the biblical framework of stewardship in chapters 1-6 and the encouragement of stewardship in a congregation in chapters 7-11.

The material can also be studied at a more leisurely pace, taking one or more chapters per session. Alternatively, this would provide an excellent focus for a council retreat. Some of the material could be dealt with by the committee of the whole. Other material will be very suitable for break-out groups. Whatever the agenda, suggestions for guiding session activities and discussion questions follow each chapter.

TAKING THE CHALLENGE

It's time to put our fears behind us—to mention the unmentionable. We need to discover stewardship as one of the key issues the church of Christ faces today. As I was entering the ministry seventeen years ago, one astute pastor said to me, "The biggest challenge the church faces is not doctrinal but practical: how will we handle our wealth?" Almost two decades of ministry have convinced me of the truth of that observation. The time to deal courageously with the financial stewardship issue has arrived.

CHAPTER 1

FOUR MYTHS ABOUT STEWARDSHIP

I f a most-misunderstood-word contest were held in Christian circles today, the word *stewardship* would certainly be in the running. Being asked to serve on a stewardship committee makes our blood run cold. It conjures up the specter of pushy people twisting the arms of reluctant givers. We are tired of people begging us for a buck, so we don't want to join the ranks of those tugging at people's wallets. For most of us stewardship is simply a euphemism for fund-raising.

Several years ago I collected and kept all the solicitations that arrived in my mailbox during the course of two weeks. The result was an intimidating stack of envelopes two inches thick. Did I take the time to read each letter carefully? Did I carefully assess the pros and cons of each organization? Hardly!

No doubt your mailbox contains a similar stack of solicitations. Is it any wonder that we eventually build an invisible sound barrier around ourselves to ward off any and all talk about stewardship? The needs of the world are so great! By comparison our resources seem so insignificant. Surrounded by so many needs, we feel guilt bubbling to the surface. No matter how much we give, we have a gnawing sense of shame about what we keep. A friend once said to me, "Must I give away *everything* I have to find peace within myself?" Who can blame our parishioners if they resist the persistent reminders of our affluence?

CHURCH LEADER UNEASE

But it isn't just parishioners who cringe at the mention of stewardship. So do many church leaders.

As a deacon you may be reading this book with a certain amount of apprehension. A year ago you were sitting in the pew, blithely unaware of your congregation's unstable financial condition. Now from your new perspective it appears that the disparity between the congregation's giving and the church budget has suddenly become your responsibility. But that's hardly fair. After all, you protest, you were not appointed to be a fund-raiser for the congregation! What's a deacon to do?

As an elder you may be feeling uneasy because concern about the budget shortfall has been rising in your council* for the past year. The deacons have pointedly asked the elders to "do something." After all, they point out, giving is a sign of spiritual health. So when it comes time to make those tough calls on nongivers, its *your* job!

You think the deacons are just passing the buck. You grouse to yourself, "How can I possibly talk to people about their giving without creating enough alienation to push them right into another church?" What's an elder to do?

As a pastor you're worried because the bills of the church keep flooding in. There isn't enough money to recarpet the nursery, let alone expand the church's ministry to the community. Now the council is clamoring for more emphasis in your preaching on the subject of giving. But every time it comes up, you feel defensive. It's not that you don't believe that giving is important. You do. It's just that you don't quite know how to approach the issue. You seriously believe the gospel is a gospel of grace. But appeals for better stewardship seem to come across as so much legalism. Laying guilt trips on your congregation isn't your thing. What's a pastor to do?

CUTTING THROUGH THE HAZE

The place to start is to expose some of the myths that surround the topic of stewardship. Although that word is often bandied about in church circles, the truth is that misinformation about stewardship abounds. Those myths often get in the way of a meaningful approach to stewardship within our congregations. The following are four deceptions that often wreak havoc with our stewardship efforts.

M Y T H #1: *The congregation's stewardship is primarily a matter of paying the church bills.*

Many of us live with the misconception that stewardship is primarily a matter of fund-raising. That's what discomforts our hapless deacons, who are convinced that their stewardship responsibility is first and foremost the raising of additional dollars for the general fund.

Let's dispel that myth right away. Stewardship does not just force us to harp relentlessly on the financial insolvency of the congregation.

---

*This term will be used throughout this book to denote a congregation's governing body made up of ministers, elders, and deacons.

Stewardship offers much wider perspectives than just the fund-raising efforts of the church.

Don't misunderstand me. I know that religious organizations, including my own congregation, need money in their corporate checkbooks. And I'm thankful for Christian fund-raisers who conduct their work with integrity and conviction. I'm grateful, too, for a new awareness throughout God's kingdom of financial resources that can be tapped for the work of Christ. I am convinced of the importance of the development office for Christian organizations of all sizes. But I'm not a fund-raiser.

So why am I writing about stewardship? It's because fund-raising for Christian organizations is only one small slice of the stewardship pie. Stewardship is first and foremost a lifestyle rooted in grace that expresses the fruit of gratitude. In *Stewardship and the Economy of God* John Reuman quotes T. A. Kantonen, who defined stewardship as "the living expression of the total content of the Christian faith" (p. 4). *Stewardship* is another word for *discipleship*, and discipleship is a way of life! Leading a congregation to discover that way of life is among the greatest privileges given by God to church leaders.

MYTH #2: *Faith and finances do not mix.*

A recent survey reveals that two-thirds of those who attend religious services each week agree with this statement: "Money is one thing, morals and values are completely separate" (Wuthnow, *God and Mammon in America*, p. 128). If you share the conviction that a grand canyon exists between morality, faith, and finances, then you will commiserate with the elder who can't figure out why someone charged with spiritual leadership should be asked to talk to a fellow member about money.

But those two-thirds of service attenders are wrong about the existence of this great divide. Faith and finances *do* mix. One-eighth of the content of the gospels deals with financial considerations. Nearly half the parables that Jesus tells relate in some way to money matters. Our Lord spends so much time talking about the subject it's obvious that for him this great divide between faith and finances does not exist.

The truth is that what we do with our dollars is an accurate reflection of our spiritual priorities. Our checkbooks say as much about our spiritual lives as they do about our personal finances. What we do with our dollars is as much a spiritual matter as whether we show up in church on Sunday morning.

MYTH #3: *Stewardship is best motivated by guilt.*

"'Stop worrying about your money, your gold and silver,' the preacher thundered. 'You can't take it with you anyway, and even if you could, it would only melt'" (Rudy, p. 9).

Is that a typical pulpit appeal to stewardship? Perhaps some preachers, especially from other traditions, warn from the pulpit, "Give more money, or with your wealth you have bought a one-way ticket to hell!" But such talk uses coercion to extract more dollars from donors. Preachers do not need to turn stewardship sermons into guilt-laden harangues for more cash. Our stewardship, like all of the Christian life, is born of grace. Unless our stewardship is rooted in grace, it will become forced and pinched—a pale reflection of what God intends it to be.

In 2 Corinthians 9:7 we read that God loves cheerful givers. The word "cheerful" is *hilaros* in the Greek text, which forms the root for our word *hilarious.* Our goal as church leaders is to raise up "hilarious" Christians who, through their gifts and offerings, are as ungrudging in their giving as our God is in sending us the Son.

MYTH #4: *Encouraging congregational stewardship is the job of (a) the pastor, (b) the elders, (c) the deacons (choose one).*

Why not add to the list: (d) all of the above. Encouraging stewardship is the task of all leaders in the church. Once we get past the myths, we discover that leading a church forward in stewardship requires a team effort.

A united stewardship effort will happen only if we stop tossing stewardship around the council room like a hot potato. Stewardship is the responsibility of deacon, elder, and pastor alike. Deacons are not elected to serve as the church's finance committee but to alleviate human need and to teach the congregation "hilarious" stewardship. Elders serve the spiritual needs of the congregation by demonstrating how spiritual realities come to expression in very physical ways, as Jesus does in Matthew 25. When pastors preach and teach the whole counsel of God, they cannot ignore the subjects of money, finance, and giving.

GETTING EARS TO HEAR

It's time to break the conspiracy of silence within our churches today, a conspiracy in which both church leaders and members participate. It's a silence about money. One survey indicates that we are least likely to discuss personal finances with members of our own congregations. Only 5 percent of us have discussed a financial matter with someone from our local church during the past year (Wuthnow, p. 140). Why? Partly because we have embraced stewardship myths rather than stewardship truth. As Christian sociologist Wuthnow concludes from this survey, "If religious leaders want to help people apply their faith to their finances . . ., it seems clear that breaking through the barrier against talking about money must be a first step" (p. 141).

This book is intended as an encouragement to you as leaders to take those initial steps that will lead your congregation to a better appreciation of how faith affects finances. That can only happen if you work together as a team, yoked in a common harness, pulling in the same direction. Only a combined effort will bring your congregation to greater maturity in the area of finance.

A team approach also helps us overcome the fear of having to go it alone, which so often pulls us back from actively promoting stewardship in our churches. We seldom feel more lonely as church leaders than when we are singled out to lead in areas of stewardship: the deacon forced to beat the financial bushes for the dollars to meet the budget; the elder coerced into making that call on a nongiving member; the pastor railroaded into a sermon on money. These unfortunate folks have something in common. They feel that the burden of the church's financial future has been suddenly dropped on their shoulders. They find that unfair.

It *is* unfair! When we must go it alone on matters of stewardship, we find ourselves climbing out on a fragile limb. When anyone complains about stewardship, our precarious perch can easily be cut off by fellow leaders. None of us need to find ourselves out on that limb. The work of teaching and encouraging financial stewardship falls to all of us. When we honor that reality, we can realistically communicate to our congregations the rich perspective of God's Word on giving. In the following chapters we will take a lingering look at that astonishing Word.

SESSION SUGGESTIONS
FOR THE LEADER

Scripture Reading: Luke 12:13-34

Invite someone to read this passage aloud. Discuss briefly what verse 21 means by being "rich towards God." Also reflect briefly on verse 34: "For where your treasure is, there your heart will be also." Perhaps you can find a good devotional on this passage to share with your group.

Quotable Quotes

If participants have not had time to read this chapter, allow them to do so now. For subsequent sessions ask them to come prepared by having read and studied the chapter(s) under discussion. Begin your discussion by providing a brief overview of the chapter. For each of the following quotes from this chapter, ask a participant to read the quote aloud and briefly explain and/or reflect on it. Allow input from the group as well.

> [Stewardship is] the living expression of the total content of the Christian faith (Reuman, p. 4).

> Stewardship is another word for discipleship, and discipleship is a way of life.

> Deacons are not elected to serve as the church's finance committee but to alleviate human need and to teach the congregation "hilarious" stewardship.

> Elders serve the spiritual needs of the congregation by demonstrating how spiritual realities come to expression in very physical ways.

> When pastors preach and teach the whole counsel of God, they cannot ignore the subjects of money, finance, and giving.

Implications and Applications

For this and subsequent sessions browse through the questions provided. Ask your group to discuss those that are meaningful to your church's context and skip those that aren't. Add your own questions and allow the group to do so as well. Ask your clerk or a reporter to jot down concrete ideas that surface during your discussion. Have him or her take note of those suggestions that may lead your council to further action in (re)structuring the way in which you can nurture your church to become a firstfruits congregation. Make sure these suggestions end up on the council's agenda.

1. Compare the terms "stewardship" and "fund-raising." What's the difference? For which are you responsible as council?

2. Do you give concrete guidance to your members about the level of financial support you expect from each of them? How much should they give? How much should they keep? How do you let them know?

3. How do you help your members sift through the barrage of financial requests they receive? How do you help them to be knowledgeable givers?

4. To what extent is financial giving a spiritual matter? Who should raise the matter with members?

5. How do you make the task of leading the congregation in stewardship a team effort? How do you hold each other accountable? How do you train new elders and deacons to do their part?

Closing Worship

Make praise to God for his rich bounty to you and your congregation the focus of your closing worship. In song and prayer focus on our provider's sustaining goodness to us. Dare to get specific about confessing ways in which you as church leaders have avoided challenging and equipping God's people to be good stewards. Pray that God will give you the courage, energy, love, and conviction to do so. Pray also that members of your congregation will be good givers who put their treasure where their heart is. Give thanks for the vitality of God's Spirit, the direction of God's Word, and the gifts you have received from your Lord to carry out your task.

Allow elders and deacons to contribute to the prayer time. Be clear on who will begin and who will conclude the prayer. Mention that times of silence that occur between prayers need not embarrass us. These are great times to talk to God silently or to reflect on the prayers that have already been offered by others.

CHAPTER 2

SEEING OURSELVES AS GOD SEES US

Certain diet books today tell you that "you are what you eat." I experience the truth of that statement whenever I discover I need to let out my belt an extra notch. Too many donuts and french fries have a way of going to "waist" on most of us!

"You are what you eat" may be a helpful dictum on which to structure a diet. Yet most of us believe that we are much more than just the proteins, fats, and carbohydrates we consume. We must be more than what we eat! If we are nothing other than complex mazes of molecules, then all purpose and meaning to life disappears.

But who are we? How shall we define ourselves? Ironically, because our world has preferred to forget God when we ask such questions, a crisis of human identity has arisen. John Calvin observes in the opening of his *Institutes* that it is in knowing God that we come to knowledge of ourselves. He is right. Only when we acknowledge that we are created for a vertical relationship with God can we come to see ourselves as God sees us: as stewards.

As I write these words, I am living in Chicago. I walk the busy streets of the Loop and pass hundreds of people on their way to shops and offices. I wonder how all these people look at themselves. Do they see themselves as insignificant cogs in the whirling wheels of industry and business? Do they see themselves as merely part of a consumer society, living to buy the next electronic toy to hit the market? If I were to ask this swirling cross-section of humanity to identify itself, would anyone tell me that he or she is a steward of God?

Even Christians do not commonly see themselves that way. As Christians we are likely to say our uniqueness lies in the fact that we bear the divine image. That's an excellent biblical answer of course. But seeing ourselves also as stewards helps us to better understand the purpose for the God-likeness stamped upon us. We are imagebearers so that we may be stewards over all the world.

THE CREATION CONTEXT

To understand stewardship, let's begin where God begins: "In the beginning God created the heavens and the earth" (Gen. 1:1). The creation story forms the backdrop for understanding the material world. God created the universe. From the start Scripture affirms the importance of our physical existence. The world was not created by malevolent forces but by the God of light, who is also God and Father of our Lord Jesus Christ. Human existence is intrinsically physical existence.

Scripture rejects any attempt to drive a wedge between the spiritual and the material. The earthy tone of Genesis 1 echoes down through the ancient Hebrew Scriptures we call the Old Testament. And the embrace of things physical continues on into the New Testament. Anyone familiar with the parables of Jesus knows that money mattered to Christ. Half the recorded events about the early church in Acts deal with material possessions (Getz, p. 107). Even the final book of the Bible assures us that God's last word on the subject of redemption is not only a "new heaven" but a "new earth." God's word on the physical creation is a resounding "Yes!"

The physical realm, as well as the spiritual, serves the purposes of God. The creation story implies that true religion embraces all dimensions of existence. Regardless of what spiritual "highs" God intends for those who worship the Ruler of heaven, the worshipers' feet remain planted firmly on the ground.

MEET THE STEWARD

It is against the backdrop of creation that we come face-to-face with God's crowning work. Adam and Eve stand in a special relationship to both the Creator and the creation. On the one hand, humanity is a special creation of God, uniquely enlivened by the very in-breathing of the Creator (Gen. 2:7) and capable of establishing true community with God. No other creature has the Godlike capacities needed to establish an I-thou relationship with the Creator.

On the other hand, Adam and Eve are not divine. They are creatures formed from the dust of the earth (Gen. 2:7). The very nature of the devil's lie is to suggest that Adam and Eve can be "like God," establishing for themselves their own ethical system of right and wrong. The curse of God upon human rebellion clearly indicates that we share in the finiteness of the rest of creation: "For dust you are and to dust you will return" (Gen. 3:19).

So you and I occupy a unique niche in the cosmos. We stand below God, yet above all else in creation. And because we are unique beings, God gives us a unique calling. While the word is not used in the early chapters of Genesis, the best term to describe our special calling is *steward.*

The English word *steward* derives from the Old English *stigweard*, which itself is a composite of *stig* ("house") and *weard* ("warden, keeper"). Webster's *New Collegiate Dictionary* defines *steward* as "one employed in a large household or estate to manage domestic concerns including supervision of servants, collection of rents, and keeping of accounts." In the Greek the steward is the *oikonomos*, the one who literally orders the household.

While Hebrew does not have a single word we translate as *steward*, the office of steward was well-known. Several times in the Old Testament we encounter the servant who represents his master and thereby assumes responsibility for his master's estate. Joseph's steward speaks with the authority of Joseph himself (Gen. 43:15-44). David's stewards have oversight of all of David's kingdom (1 Chron. 27:25-31).

The office of steward is not only one of great responsibility but also of great accountability. Stewards have no inherent authority of their own. Their authority is entrusted to them by their master; if the master is displeased with a servant's oversight, the steward can be replaced with another (Isa. 22:15-22).

STILL STEWARDS

Today we do not commonly see ourselves as *stigweards*. Yet the essence of the office is still with us. Several months ago my father-in-law was admitted to the hospital for serious surgery. The admitting nurse gave us a folder filled with some very important forms. We needed to fill them out if Dad wanted to entrust us with power-of-attorney. In case Dad was not able to make decisions for himself, he would empower his children to make them for him.

Such power-of-attorney is a remarkable trust. It can put matters of life and death in the hands of another. If Dad chose to fill out those papers, he would have made us stewards over his hospital care, stewards of his very life!

That's awesome. And that is the kind of role God has given to us. Our Creator has granted us power-of-attorney over the creation. It is this relationship that comes to glorious expression in Genesis 1:28: "Fill the earth and subdue it. Rule over the fish of the sea and the birds of the air and over every living creature that moves on the ground" (Gen. 1:28).

This "cultural mandate," as it has been called, uses remarkably strong language. The verb translated "have dominion" means literally "to tread." The verb translated "subdue" was used to describe the work of subjecting enemy nations (Stott, p. 124). This authority is also underscored by Adam's responsibility to name the animals (Gen. 2:19-20). In Scripture naming is more than giving a label. It refers to an acknowledgment of the essential nature of what is being named. Adam's commission to name the animals demonstrates the same authority that stewards exercise.

CALLED TO ACCOUNT

But is our dominion-bearing without boundaries? Are Adam and Eve allowed to do as they please? No. Like all stewards, Adam and Eve remain responsible to their Lord. That's the very implication of our image-bearing:

> *Just as powerful earthly kings, to indicate their claim to dominion, erect an image of themselves in the provinces of their empire where they do not personally appear, so man is placed upon earth in God's image as God's sovereign emblem. He is really only God's representative summoned to maintain and enforce God's claim to dominion over the earth.*

> —*von Rad,* Genesis: A Commentary,
> The Old Testament Library, *p. 60*

Genesis 2:15 underscores Adam's responsibility to God. God places him in the garden "to work it and take care of it." The Hebrew verbs used here are *abad,* which can be translated "be a slave to," and *shamar,* which can be translated "preserve." These words describe actions that Adam performs for the benefit of the garden. Like Adam, we must exercise our stewardship with an eye to all creation.

In situations where my aged father puts his future into my hands, the possibility always exists that I may exploit his trust. If I do not want the responsibility of caring for him, I may decide against medical procedures that probably should be performed. Or like the prodigal son, I may want my inheritance now. But responsible stewardship demands that every choice I make be motivated by a concern for my father, who now cannot make medical decisions for himself. If I am a faithful steward, I must be driven by a healthy commitment to the one who has placed himself under my care.

So it is with our role as stewards in God's world. Exploitation is ruled out. God did not entrust us with the world for the sake of self-aggrandizement. God placed it under our care so that we would allow the potentialities of creation to emerge for God's glory. Implicit in our stewardly identity is a very healthy, Christian ecology.

When we consider the biblical givens, we can see that the term *steward* accurately defines our human identity even though the word is not explicitly used in the opening chapters of Genesis. Douglas Hall remarks that the notion of stewardship *at once tells us something about the no and the yes of human identity in relationship: No, Adam and Eve are not masters. Yes, they are types of servants. But no, Adam and Eve are not just slaves, mechanical puppets, or robots. Yes, they are responsible and accountable to others. No, Adam or Eve is not just one of the other creatures, but yes, they are also like the others.*

—*Hall,* The Steward: A Biblical Symbol Come of Age, *p. 31*

THE STEWARD'S FALL

It's been said that humanity today lives "east of Eden." The fall into sin can only be described as insurrection.

What is the impact of the fall upon our God-given vocation of steward? Think in a new way of the pride that motivated the first sin. Think of it as rejection of the role of steward. Adam and Eve seek to exchange responsible stewardship for autonomy. The stewards try to usurp the position of the Master. Tempted to become "like God," Adam and Eve set their own course for the creation. They decide for themselves what is good or evil in the world about them. The result? Disaster! Sin not only creates disharmony between steward and Lord but also between steward and creation:

> *Cursed is the ground because of you;*
> *through painful toil you will eat of it*
> *all the days of your life.*
> *It will produce thorns and thistles for you,*
> *and you will eat the plants of the field.*

> —*Genesis 3:17-18*

From now on the created order will resist humankind's efforts at faithful stewardship. This resistance is due both to an intrinsic change within the creation itself and to our fallen tendency to work at cross-purposes with the creation. God literally says, "Cursed is the ground to you." When we refuse to cooperate with nature, its good things can become a curse. So we build houses on hills in California where mud slides will inevitably sweep them to ruin. We pour more waste into our rivers than our waterways can possibly purify. We suffer the consequences of living in a beautiful world we have turned ugly. As we work against creation, creation inflicts its penalties on us.

TOO LITTLE, TOO MUCH

Sin has significantly distorted our very perception of the created order. Paradoxically, that distortion moves us in opposite directions—simultaneously we make too little of creation and too much.

In one way we make too little of it. God tells Eve and Adam that part of the curse will be Adam's lording over his wife. But it is not just woman that man tends to lord over but also the entire created order. He replaces stewardship with exploitation. The cultural mandate now becomes an excuse to bring creation to its knees for the sake of self-aggrandizement. The caring has gone out of humanity's dominion.

In another way we make too much of creation. Human beings have a tendency to deify themselves and also the material world in which they live. And so the irony arises: the very objects of human stewardship threaten to become their lords and gods. Wanting to master wealth, they are instead mastered by wealth.

How desperately we need to be set free from the consequences of our own muddling failure and sin!

THE STEWARD REDEEMED

Can fallen stewards be redeemed? Or has God given up hope that we can be useful as our Creator works out cosmic purposes? The good news comes to us in a remarkable way: Jesus' own readiness to name his disciples as kingdom stewards. In Luke 12, for example, Christ relates a parable in which he reminds us that serious stewards must always remain watchful and ready for their master's return. The role of steward, implicitly given to God's people in the Old Testament, is now explicitly applied to God's New Testament people. Fallen stewards can be restored to their rightful place in their Master's house.

But that restoration can only happen through the one whom we might call the great steward, Jesus Christ. Christian tradition often speaks of Christ's ministry as fulfilling the offices of prophet, priest, and king. Can we also speak of Christ fulfilling the office of steward? Against the backdrop of Scripture, we certainly can. Christ's ministry uniquely expresses his role as steward of God's grace. Christ is not only *the Son of God* but also *the Servant of God*, who has fulfilled a mediatorial role between God and the cosmos.

As a faithful steward, Christ has come not to do his own will but God's will (John 5:30). As a good steward, Christ directs his ministry outward in service to the creation. Christ becomes the great exemplar of stewardship. Hall notes,

> *Because he is a just and faithful steward ... he desires nothing for himself. Because he is obedient to the one he represents, he is not concerned*

about saving his own life, but lays it down for his friends. He does not think in terms of possession, not even the possession of his own life.

—Hall, p. 43

Christ's ministry of stewardship once again makes ours possible. It's important that we recognize that fact. Unless we take seriously Christ's stewardship, our calling as stewards becomes separated from the gospel. True stewardship for the New Testament believer grows from grace. It recognizes that "all are yours, and you are of Christ, and Christ is of God" (1 Cor. 3:22-23). In Christ we are taken up into his stewardship (Hall, p. 44).

Only if we understand the relationship between Christ's stewardship and ours, will we free it from a legalistic stranglehold and lift it into the arena of grace. Stewardship becomes an expression of the wonderful freedom we have in Christ. Again Hall says it well:

The law of stewardship, which many of us know to be true enough, insists that human beings must be faithful trustees of the life of the world. But it is one thing to know this and another to do it. The gospel of stewardship begins by overcoming that within us which prevents our being stewards—the pride of imagining ourselves owners, the sloth of irresponsibility, neglect, and apathy. And that gospel gives us the grace and courage that we need to exercise a love that is larger than our self-esteem or our anxiety about ourselves.

—Hall, p. 44

SERVING NOW, SERVING THEN

For God's redeemed people, stewardship begins with an understanding that we are preeminently "entrusted with the secret things of God" (1 Cor. 4:1). The gospel itself is the highest trust given to us as stewards. It renews us and gives us a fresh opportunity to fulfill the cultural mandate of Genesis 1. The church of Jesus Christ is the steward of that reconciliation in the world today.

Unless the church takes seriously its vocation as steward of God's grace, the broader stewardship of God's creation will not be restored. It is redeeming grace that empowers us to live as stewards over all that which God entrusts to us. Christ's redemptive work extends beyond our personal salvation to embrace heaven and earth (Rev. 21:1). Our concerns should be just as broad. The day will come when we will be stewards of that new heaven and earth. We prepare for that future role by serving as faithful stewards today.

SESSION SUGGESTIONS
FOR THE LEADER

Scripture Reading: Genesis 1:26-30; Colossians 3:1-17

Ask volunteers to read these two passages aloud. Discuss briefly how, according to Genesis, we image God. Reread Colossians 3:9-10 and discuss what this "new self" is, which is "being renewed in knowledge in the image of its Creator."

Quotable Quotes

Assume that participants have read the chapter. If your experience shows that's not the case, exhort them to greater obedience, perhaps by suggesting that those who have not done their homework get to clean up the coffee cups. Begin your discussion by providing a brief overview of the chapter. Ask participants to take turns reading each of the following quotes from this chapter aloud, briefly explaining and/or reflecting on them. Allow the group to respond.

> *No, Adam and Eve are not masters. Yes, they are types of servants. But no, Adam and Eve are not just slaves, mechanical puppets, or robots. Yes, they are responsible and accountable to others. No, Adam or Eve is not just one of the other creatures, but yes, they are also like the others (Hall, p. 31).*

> *Just as powerful earthly kings, to indicate their claim to dominion, erect an image of themselves in the provinces of their empire where they do not personally appear, so man is placed upon earth in God's image as God's sovereign emblem. He is really only God's representative, summoned to maintain and enforce God's claim to dominion over the earth (von Rad, p. 60).*

> *Sin not only creates disharmony between steward and Lord but also between steward and creation.*

> *Human beings have a tendency to deify themselves and also the material world in which they live. And so the irony arises: the very objects of human stewardship threaten to become their lords and gods. Wanting to master wealth, they are instead mastered by wealth.*

> *For God's redeemed people, stewardship begins with an understanding that we are preeminently "entrusted with the secret things of God" (1 Cor. 4:1). The gospel itself is the highest trust given to us as stewards. It renews us and gives us a fresh opportunity to fulfill the cultural mandate of Genesis 1.*

Implications and Applications

Discuss the questions you find helpful. Give precedence to those you or your group may have. Record concrete ideas of issues that your council will need to address in providing leadership in the area of stewardship.

1.   Read James 1:27. Does this text support Heerspink's conclusion that "true religion embraces all dimensions of existence"? What practical application does that have for you as spiritual leaders?

2.   What is a steward? How are all human beings stewards? How can we help our members be good stewards?

3.   What has sin done to our stewardship? In what ways do we make too little of creation? In what ways do we make too much of it?

4.   Is Heerspink right to suggest that Jesus fills not only the offices of prophet, priest, and king but also of steward? Explain.

5.   If we as redeemed Christians continue to be stewards, how should we concretely fulfil that task? How can we help our members fulfil theirs?

Closing Worship

A song or two relating to our role as stewards would provide a fitting bridge from study to prayer. In your closing prayer ask God's forgiveness for ways your church has neglected its stewardship role. In particular confess the ways in which you as church leaders may not have provided appropriate leadership in that area. Pray for God's wisdom and guidance in fulfilling that responsibility. Pray particularly for courage. You'll need it as you give leadership to the congregation as a whole and to members individually! Give thanks for the many resources God has given your church. Offer praise for God's daily care for each of you.

CHAPTER 3

PENNIES FROM HEAVEN OR FILTHY LUCRE?

People who like to view wealth and opulence can indulge their voyeuristic cravings with a television show called "Lifestyles of the Rich and Famous." I don't watch much television. But when I happen upon this program while channel surfing, I confess that I catch a few clips. I too am tempted to participate vicariously in a lifestyle I can't afford. The show is supposed to be about the rich and *famous*. But we are much more interested in the money than the notoriety. Why would we be interested in a movie star who lives a plain, middle-class lifestyle like us? We want to see how rich people spend money in ways we never even dream about. Down deep we are tempted to believe Alan Alda, who declares, "It isn't necessary to be rich and famous to be happy. It's only necessary to be rich" (Myers, *The Pursuit of Happiness*, p. 32).

I'm writing these lines while on sabbatical, staying in an apartment owned by a Chicago church. This church has practiced a common purse for the past thirty years. As I rub shoulders with these fine Christians, I feel rather guilty that my wife and I typically buy new clothes for our children instead of going to secondhand stores. I refrain from mentioning the places we go to on vacation or the restaurants we visit while we're here in Chicago. I am almost embarrassed to be driving around in our own van. After all, these folks *share* cars! How would I feel if we had brought along *both* of our vehicles from Michigan?

All of these thoughts add to my confusion about how to deal with money. I am uncomfortable with the lifestyle of those rich people who use their money to outdo their equally wealthy neighbors. I am equally uncomfortable with the lifestyle of those who intentionally impoverish themselves for the sake of God's kingdom. I question whether my solid, middle-class income should make me feel guilty or blessed. My struggle is really a search for a theological answer to the nature of wealth. What does the Bible say about money anyway?

TWO EXTREMES

In *God, Revelation, and Authority* Carl F. H. Henry points out that our current struggle to understand our world comes into sharp focus when set against the philosophies of ancient times. In recent years we have revisited the questions they posed about culture. Ancient Greek philosophy presented two radically opposing views of what constituted reality.

First, there was the viewpoint of Democritus (c. 460-370 B.C.), who was a blatant materialist. Democritus argued that reality consisted only of atoms in motion. The gods themselves were only beings whose atoms were of a higher quality than the ones possessed by ordinary mortals like us. For Democritus, everything was reducible to the physical aspect of reality.

The ghost of Democritus haunts our secular culture in the raw naturalism that sweeps through society. Many people believe that physical reality is all there is. Human behavior is reducible to nothing more than physical drives. Love becomes raw sex. The good life becomes the gratification of physical cravings. "Lifestyles of the Rich and Famous" becomes the sole standard for that good life.

But the materialism of Democritus didn't sit well with the influential philosophers who followed. Plato (427-347 B.C.) and Aristotle (384-322 B.C.) had the sense to see that materialism offers no purpose to human existence. Without a sense of meaning, civilization as we know it becomes an impossibility. The alternative they offered was idealism. Not the physical, but the spiritual is the "really real." The mind and the world of ideas are eternal. Truth and "the good" are never changing.

It's not surprising that our culture has also seen the pendulum swing against naturalism in the form of the New Age movement. While they exhibit much diversity in their beliefs, New Agers want to take seriously the realm of the spirit. For many of them, spiritual realities are the essence of existence.

WHICH WAY?

Materialism and idealism constitute the horns of the dilemma on which I as a Christian seem to be caught. It is difficult not to feel pulled in one direction or the other. Should I move toward a "health-and-wealth gospel"? Should I believe the preachers who assure me that having what I want materially is the obvious sign that God is blessing me? Should I believe that God wants to give me wealth? Is it only my lack of faith that stops a wonderful financial flow into my bank account?

Or should I turn away from everything beyond the mere necessities of life? Am I called to a lifestyle of simplicity, as some Christians suggest?

Must I consider all delights in the things of this earth to be improper and a denial that my real treasure is in heaven?

To put it in everyday language: may I eat steak as well as salad? May I drive a Buick as well as pedal a bicycle? May I buy a brand-name sport coat as well as hand-me-downs from the secondhand shops? May I be a materialistic Christian and still be Christ's disciple? The answer to these questions lies in a careful examination of Scripture to discover a way out of my dilemma.

THE GOODNESS OF THE CREATION

"God saw all that he had made, and it was very good" (Gen. 1:31). We are so familiar with the opening verses of Genesis that we no longer marvel at these shocking words. The opening verses of the Bible take to task both extremes of materialism and idealism. "God saw all that he had made"—no God composed of refined atoms here. Between Creator and creation there is an infinite, qualitative difference. God calls into existence the physical world. A philosophy arguing that the world of matter is all that exists spouts nonsense. Genesis teaches an obvious spiritual-physical duality.

"And it was very good"—with those words Scripture dismisses an idealism that scorns the material world. There is no rejection of the physical. God declares the cosmos good. All that God has made is rightly ordered and fulfills its proper purpose (von Rad, *Genesis: A Commentary*, p. 52). From the stars that course through the sky to the fish that swim in the sea, the various parts of creation fit together like a finely tuned engine. Each part strains for a common purpose—to sing the glory of its Maker. Creation achieves the fullness of its purpose as God sits back to delight in it.

This means that the physical realm is a fitting stage on which we can live as stewards before our Maker. It's no surprise that the Scriptures are filled with passages that affirm our right to use and delight in abundant, physical blessings. God never reprimanded Abraham, Job, David, or Solomon for being wealthy. We meet rich believers on the pages of the New Testament as well. In his letter to Timothy Paul adds special instructions to rich members of the church in Ephesus (1 Tim. 6:17).

THE LIGHT SIDE

The Bible introduces us to a host of wealthy God-fearers. But it does more. It reveals that God calls the Old Testament people of Israel to experience physical blessings. Canaan is not merely an adequate country with a minimal living standard; it is a land flowing with milk and honey. True, the abundance of Canaan is symbolic of a greater country to come. Still,

God was comfortable using the lavish physical blessings of Canaan to teach people about the riches of divine grace.

In *Freedom of Simplicity*, Richard Foster describes these physical blessings as the "light side of money." That side emerges repeatedly from the pages of Scripture. We need not reject material abundance in order to prove our sainthood. Gold, silver, and "the cattle on a thousand hills" (Ps. 50:10) belong to God. God's possessions cannot be inherently evil.

We discover that God allows people and nations to possess great wealth. Yet we note a strange tension in the lives of many rich God-fearers. Abraham may be wealthy, but he never personally experiences the abundance of the land God promises him. All the real estate he ever owns in Canaan is the grave where he buries his beloved Sarah. Job is incredibly affluent. But he loses all his wealth during a time of intense testing. Israel receives the land of Canaan but endures forty years of trial in the wilderness. All these episodes imply that there is more to the life of faith than just an unthinking embrace of wealth as a sure sign of God's favor.

THE OTHER SIDE OF MONEY

What's the other side of physical abundance? Let's return to the moment when Israel is about to enter Canaan. We find the Israelites in high spirits. They feel like a birthday child when, after waiting an eternity, the big day finally arrives. Only Moses has the audacity to throw cold water on their celebration. In today's language he says something like this:

> *When you have enjoyed the best society has to offer you, praise the Lord from whom it came. Don't forget your God. Obey God's commands. Otherwise, after you've dined at the finest restaurants and built houses in the best part of town, after your stock portfolios have grown fat and your business interests have become the envy of the community, then your heart will become proud, and you will forget the Lord your God who saved you. You will say, "I've got what it takes to make good. My hard work has produced this wealth for me."*

> —Deuteronomy 8, author's paraphrase

Who needs this warning? We do, as much as Israel. According to Moses something about money inspires pride. Adam and Eve's original sin was their pride in thinking they could be like their Maker. Moses suggests that pride grows as wealth multiplies. Wealth tempts us to think that the strength of our own hands has produced it.

Consequently, we are faced with what Richard Foster calls "the dark side of money." Modern culture ignores this shadow. I remember vividly a conversation I had with a businessman who argued passionately for the moral neutrality of money. He would have liked the dictionary to define money as "something generally accepted as a medium of exchange." If that is all money is, then it should yield easily to our efforts to domesticate and tame it. Our Western culture assumes that money is just a secularized commodity we can study objectively, using the scientific principles of economics.

It may come as a surprise to many Westerners that this view of money is rather naive. A study of money in the history of our world indicates that culture after culture recognized that money is more than a medium of exchange, providing discussion fodder for the economist. It is a reality fraught with religious power, which we need to treat with awesome respect. Robert Wuthnow writes,

> *Mesoamerican religions taught that money had a soul and should be exchanged only after prayer and fasting. When money consisted of precious metals, the mining of these metals was often surrounded by religious rites. In Sumatra, for example, other metals could not be carried into the gold mines, lest the spirit of gold flee. The Dyaks of Borneo believed the soul of the gold sought revenge on those who mined it.*

> —*Wuthnow,* God and Mammon in America, *p. 118*

Not the social scientist but the shaman needed to be consulted on money matters!

THAT'S THE LIFE?

Our culture scoffs at such superstitions. We have demythologized gold and silver. In the process we have made it difficult to hear the Bible's message about the danger of wealth. Scripture insists that money as a complex reality needs to be addressed not only by economic theory but also by religious conviction. Why? Consider Christ's own analysis. In Luke 12:15 Jesus illuminates the danger of wealth: "life does not consist in the abundance of possessions" (NRSV).

The problem with money is that it is too easily associated with life. As I browse through the travel section of the newspaper, dozens of different destinations pop out at me. They all offer me the "time of my life." If only I had the money, I could "live it up" at exotic destinations ranging from the Caribbean to the French Riviera. Money scratches my materialistic itch.

But money can buy more than cars and homes and luxury vacations. It can even buy intangible things. It can buy reputation. Acts 5 reports the story of Ananias and Sapphira. They sell a piece of property and pocket part of the income. Then they imply that they have put all of the proceeds at the disposal of the apostles because they think that generous, sacrificial giving can buy them a reputation for piety.

Money can also buy power. The film *Indecent Proposal* explored the raw power of wealth. A couple in financial straits needs money desperately. A wealthy acquaintance offers the couple a million dollars if they agree to allow him to go to bed with the wife. The film is ostensibly about sex. But it deals with something more—money and the power that money can buy. These three—sex, money, and power—are intimately related. As Richard Foster observes, "Money manifests itself as power. Sex is used to acquire both money and power. And power is often called 'the best aphrodisiac'" (p. 2).

We're faced with the paradoxical nature of money. On the one hand, our possessions are evidence of God's rich blessing. On the other hand, those same possessions feed the delusion that we don't need God. Our riches have a way of turning into surrogate gods to which we willingly sell our souls.

INESCAPABLE EVIDENCE

How does this deifying of riches show itself? The great Physician lays a finger on a key symptom—anxiety: "Therefore I tell you, do not worry about your life, what you will eat; or about your body, what you will wear. Life is more than food, and the body more than clothes" (Luke 12:22-23).

Our culture argues that there is no connection between money and true spirituality. But anxiety over money betrays us. Money—or perhaps the lack of it—is one of the great roots of anxiety in our culture. Eighty-eight percent of Americans wish they had more money. Seventy-two percent worry about paying their bills (Wuthnow, p. 135). And it isn't just the lower class that struggles with such fears. Of the richest third of Americans, 39 percent fret about meeting their financial obligations. Financial anxiety is not limited to any single stratum of society.

Some of us lived through the Great Depression. We remember times when we literally did not have a dollar to our name. Such poverty intimidates us to this day. We keep a nest-egg safely tucked away in investment certificates in a federally insured institution. We're terrified that our money will run out before we die. Anxiety over money eats us up.

Others of us are baby boomers. We have no experience with economic depression. We do not share the fear of depleting our savings. We have no savings to deplete! We are consumed with concern about meeting next month's credit-card payment. Should our careers stumble, we will be in deep financial waters. Money worries gnaw at us continually.

Maybe some of us have more than we need even for an upper-class lifestyle. We have small fortunes invested in stocks and bonds. And that's our trouble! We grab the newspaper every morning and turn anxiously to the business section. Our comfortable retirement hinges upon upward trends in the market. Our brokers assure us that over time all should be well. But what if the "bears" take permanent control of Wall Street? We worry about money as if it were our child.

WHOM OR WHAT DO WE TRUST?

Jesus points out that our anxiety betrays us. It reveals that money has become our god. Jesus gives classic expression to that temptation when he declares, "You cannot serve both God and Money" (Matt. 6:24). The word for "money" in the Greek text is "mammon." It describes material possessions and implies "that in which one trusts" (*The New International Dictionary of New Testament Theology*, Vol. II, p. 837). Here lurks the precise danger underlying all our possessions. We must not trust the *creature* but the *Creator* (Matt. 6:25-33). Yet when our possessions gain the upper hand, it's in them that we lodge our trust.

This danger is very real. Ancient Israel's history depicts a people who repeatedly place their trust and confidence in everything but the Lord its God. Israel seldom heeds Moses' warning in Deuteronomy 8. And the danger remains today. Do we really take Jesus seriously when he warns how hard it will be for rich people to enter the kingdom of God? Do we really believe that Jesus means it when he tells the rich young ruler to free himself from his false god by giving all he has to the poor?

IN PURSUIT OF FINANCIAL FREEDOM

Today most people define financial freedom as being so well off financially that all their worries about the future are dispelled. Jesus' teachings make it obvious that such financial freedom is a myth. Not only do moth and rust consume our treasures on earth, but our mortality shows how ludicrous the notion is that we ever have enough to say to ourselves, "Soul, take your ease" (Luke 12).

Biblically understood, financial freedom is not a matter of achieving the point at which interest from investments exceeds living expenses. It has little to do with how affluent we are. Those people no longer enslaved by the god of riches who so cruelly dominated their lives are blessed with true financial freedom!

How do we achieve that kind of freedom? We who live affluent lifestyles are quick to point out that the Bible does not identify *money* as the root of all evil but only the *love of money*. Living in a wealthy country, we take comfort in knowing that our attitudes toward wealth, not our money itself, play the deciding role.

The Bible acknowledges that that's true. Wealth is no more a sign of an unregenerate heart than poverty is a sign of spirituality. We can earn little and be materialists. We can have much and yet live as if the things of this world are of no consequence. The Bible recognizes that from the heart emerge the core convictions of life.

Yet we must be careful. When it comes to money, it's so easy to separate attitude from action. Scripture holds the two together. When we crucify our inner love of money, outward acts of compassion and giving rise to the surface.

ACT SHREWDLY, ACT NOW!

In Luke 16 Jesus tells a most unusual parable. It's about a crooked steward who gets in trouble with his master. He's in so much hot water that he hears through the grapevine that he's about to be fired. At first he's desperate. If he loses his job, where will he turn? But then he devises a shrewd plan. He calls in his master's creditors and cuts a deal with each one, telling them that if they settle with him now, they will reduce their debt.

To the astonishment and gratitude of the community, the steward exercises a largesse never before seen in the village. Overnight he becomes the most popular man in town. Things are going to turn out all right for him after all. Once he loses his job, there will be dozens of people in the village who owe him a favor. Everyone will be his friend.

We expect that when the master hears what the steward has done, he will be furious! The steward's behavior has only confirmed the master's worst suspicions. Yet the master cannot help but admire the ingenuity with which his steward has gained the upper hand. He can only commend the steward for his shrewdness.

MAKING FRIENDS

Naturally we have a hard time understanding what this parable is doing in the New Testament. Does Jesus encourage dishonesty? No. Listen to the conclusion Jesus draws: "I tell you, use worldly wealth to gain friends for yourselves, so that when it is gone, you will be welcomed into eternal dwellings" (Luke 16:9).

Jesus commends the way this man uses economic means for noneconomic purposes. It makes no financial sense to reduce the loans made to his master. His master's dealings are now awash in red ink. But the good graces these dealings create toward the steward are priceless.

Jesus suggests that the steward sets a pattern we should follow. There are things more precious than gold. Citizens of God's kingdom know that well. Like the steward we should use economic means for noneconomic ends. We should use our resources for kingdom purposes. We should invest our money in treasures that cannot be eaten by moths or corroded by rust. One way we can do that is by giving to the work of God's kingdom. Then we gain friends who will welcome us into eternal dwellings.

GIVE IT AWAY

Do you give financial support to a halfway house for drug addicts? Do you contribute to a mission effort in the Philippines? Do you help to underwrite the salary of a Wycliffe Bible translator in Colombia? It's highly unlikely that you will ever meet in this world the people you are touching through those gifts. But when Christ receives you into eternal dwellings, you will find a welcome party at the gates.

You may find that strange because you will not recognize those who gather around. Then they will say, "You helped me kick my drug habit"; "You introduced me to Christ"; "You placed into my hands the Word of God written in my language." Then we'll all understand that we made friends we never even knew we had. Our financial support of God's kingdom work changed these people's lives for eternity.

Certainly our attitude toward money is important, but so is our behavior. Unless we learn to take some of our financial resources and give them away, we have not broken the stranglehold of mammon in our lives. Cheerful, generous giving demonstrates that money is no longer our god.

Giving becomes an act of obedience by which we affirm our identity and calling. But we need to say more. We can give out of suspicious motives. The way we give often leaves much to be desired. And the question of how much to give has echoed through the church for two thousand years. In chapter 4 we'll consider what the Bible really tells us about our giving.

SESSION SUGGESTIONS
FOR THE LEADER

Scripture Reading: Mark 10:17-31

Ask a volunteer to read this passage. Briefly discuss what Jesus means in his parable about the camel. Notice his emphatic repetition in verses 23-24 of the difficulty the rich face. Notice also the equally emphatic repetition in verse 27. There's something very important going on here—what is it? Kick this around a few minutes; then move on. The issue will reemerge later.

Quotable Quotes

After providing a brief overview, ask some participants to explain and reflect on the following quotes. Invite the group to respond.

> *I am uncomfortable with the lifestyle of those rich people who use their money to outdo their equally wealthy neighbors. I am equally uncomfortable with the lifestyle of those who intentionally impoverish themselves for the sake of God's kingdom. I question whether my solid, middle-class income should make me feel guilty or blessed. My struggle is really a search for a theological answer to the nature of wealth.*

> *Materialism and idealism constitute the horns of the dilemma on which I as a Christian seem to be caught. It is difficult not to feel pulled in one direction or the other.*

> *We're faced with the paradoxical nature of money. On the one hand, our possessions are evidence of God's rich blessing. On the other hand, those same possessions feed the delusion that we don't need God. Our riches have a way of turning into surrogate gods to which we willingly sell our souls.*

> *Our culture argues that there is no connection between money and true spirituality. But anxiety over money betrays us. Money—or perhaps the lack of it—is one of the great roots of anxiety in our culture.*

> *Unless we learn to take some of our financial resources and give them away, we have not broken the stranglehold of mammon in our lives. Cheerful, generous giving demonstrates that money is no longer our god.*

Implications and Applications

Follow the process of previous sessions: use these questions as a way to structure your discussion if you find that useful. Give priority to your own questions and those that emerge from the group.

1. What's the biblical antidote to materialism? To idealism?

2. Is material wealth a blessing from God or a curse? Does God want us all to be rich? Should we keep more than the basic necessities of life?

3. What are the light and the dark sides of wealth? What comfort and warning should we derive from them?

4. Of what sickness is anxiety about money a symptom? How should we deal with it?

5. Describe true financial freedom. How can we achieve it?

6. What does Jesus' parable of the unjust steward teach us? How shall we follow its advice? How can we encourage the people we lead to do the same?

Closing Worship

In closing worship and prayer give praise and thanks to God for material as well as spiritual blessings. You may want to read responsively an appropriate psalm. Seek God's sustaining care to keep you from wandering after the god mammon. The urgency of this petition becomes clear when we realize that in biblical terms people with roofs over their heads and enough resources to get through today and tomorrow are wealthy. Confess your anxiety about money. Promise God you will strive for greater financial freedom. Ask for a rich measure of the Holy Spirit to gain it.

CHAPTER 4

GIVING: OLD TESTAMENT FOUNDATIONS

Sometimes a single question covers a lot of theological ground. A question I often ask in church education classes looks easy: how were God's people saved in Old Testament times? The common answer I receive is that they kept the law. Then my respondent often adds with a wry smile, "Good thing that today we are saved by grace!"

That response makes me wonder if anyone really listens to the preamble to the Ten Commandments: "I am the LORD your God, who brought you out of Egypt, out of the land of slavery" (Ex. 20:2). The entire relationship between God and Israel rested upon a foundation of grace. Undeserved mercy shown to a slave people formed Abraham's descendants into a nation. The Exodus constitutes the key Old Testament event in salvation history. By that unparalleled deed God created the people who were to respond to all they had received by giving freely in return.

Our assessment of Israel's giving patterns is woefully off the mark if we think that Israel gave in order to receive divine love. For Israel giving was supposed to be a sign of gratitude, just as it is for us. That fact suggests that we should explore Old Testament giving patterns to see what they can teach us even today.

THE OLD TESTAMENT TITHE

The willing surrender to God of what we consider ours has always been part of religious life. In the first chapters of Genesis we already discover that worship is accompanied by the presentation of sacrifices. Cain and Abel both bring their offerings to God (Gen. 4:3). The text implies that both these offerings were presentations of firstfruits. So from the beginning of recorded time worshipers come to God with gifts in hand. The story also indicates that more is involved in bringing homage to God than merely presenting an offering. The attitude of the heart is as important as the gift presented.

The *tithe* is first mentioned in the life of Abram. A lightning raid on Lot's kidnappers ends in his release. Abram gratefully presents a tenth of the plunder to Melchizedek, king of Salem, "priest of God Most High" (Gen. 14:18). While Abram's gift was probably voluntary, his action wasn't unique for his day. A few chapters later the tithe resurfaces. Jacob barters with God and promises to return a tenth to the Lord in return for God's care and blessing (Gen. 28:22).

Centuries later the law of Moses formally incorporates the tithe into the economic pattern God sets for the covenant people. As the structure of the book of Deuteronomy indicates, Israel is the vassal of the great Suzerain king, Yahweh. It is only right and fitting that Israel's people bring tribute to their supreme sovereign. The tithe constitutes a significant part of that tribute.

THAT'S NOT ALL

What we have discovered so far about the tithe is clear. But we must be careful not to assume too much. As twentieth-century readers we tend to think of the tithe as a flat 10 percent ecclesiastical tax. We view it as a legalistic device devoid of grace. But Scripture reveals a very different picture.

We may be surprised to learn how complex the Old Testament legislation concerning the tithe really is. Jewish rabbis argued that the Old Testament demands three different tithes. Two of them must be brought yearly. The first stipulates a tenth of the fruit of fields and flocks: " 'A tithe of everything from the land, whether grain from the soil or fruit from the trees, belongs to the LORD; it is holy to the LORD. . . . The entire tithe of the herd and flock—every tenth animal that passes under the shepherd's rod—will be holy to the LORD' " (Lev. 27: 30, 32).

Worshipers must take the second tithe, the festival tithe, to the temple: "Be sure to set aside a tenth of all that your fields produce each year" (Deut. 14:22). God commands the third tithe to be brought every third year: "At the end of every three years, bring all the tithes of that year's produce and store it in your towns" (Deut. 14:28). If this understanding of three tithes is correct, then the Israelites did not give 10 percent but, on average, 23-1/3 percent of their income every year!

While some Jewish commentators argue that three distinct tithes are intended, more likely these various texts on the tithe overlap with one another. They probably call for one basic tithe which must be put to various uses, spelling out three of them.

DIFFERENT DESTINATIONS

The first use of the tithe supports the Old Testament priestly ministry. The Levites had no allotment of land, so they had no visible means of financial support. Their presence clearly reminds the Israelites that they were once a landless people, wandering as sojourners in the wilderness. The very existence of the Levitical priesthood gives them a sign that life ultimately depends on God's grace, not on the land's potential. So how will the Levites receive their support? God commands, "Bring all the tithes ... so that the Levites (who have no allotment or inheritance of their own) ... may come and eat and be satisfied" (Deut. 14:28-29). The tithe supports Israel's organized ministry.

A second use of the tithe provides benevolence ministry. It fills the needs of "the aliens, the fatherless, and the widows who live in [their] towns" (Deut. 14:29). Note who leads that list. Benevolence in Israel extends beyond support of its own widows and orphans. The tithe must supply the alien too. God's people must remember that what the alien now is, every Israelite once was: "Do not oppress an alien; you yourselves know how it feels to be aliens, because you were aliens in Egypt" (Ex. 23:9). The tithe provides a way by which the powerless and disenfranchised experienced the care of God.

The third use of the tithe is the most surprising: it finances a celebration of God's grace:

> Eat the tithe of your grain, new wine and oil, and the firstborn of your herds and flocks in the presence of the LORD your God at the place he will choose as a dwelling for his Name, so that you may learn to revere the LORD your God always. But if that place is too distant and you have been blessed by the LORD your God and cannot carry your tithe (because the place where the LORD will choose to put his Name is so far away), then exchange your tithe for silver, and take the silver with you and go to the place the LORD your God will choose. Use the silver to buy whatever you like: cattle, sheep, wine or other fermented drink, or anything you wish. Then you and your household shall eat there in the presence of the LORD your God and rejoice.
>
> —Deuteronomy 14:23-26

Here we find an unexpected use of the tithe. It furnishes the financial base for Israel to keep festival before the Lord. This use of the tithe was so important that Israelites were even allowed to convert their tithe from flock and field into cash so that they could travel more easily to the "place where the LORD will choose to put his Name" (14:24).

In this context I can imagine the raised eyebrows of those who object when the church budget includes such line items as "church picnic."

Shouldn't we pay for our fried chicken out of our own pockets? Some people don't find such a line item at all worthy of the church of Christ.

I have no objection to passing the hat at the picnic to pay for our chicken and potato salad. But I wonder whether our complaints might be a subtle sign that we have difficulty receiving graciously from a giving God. When it comes time to celebrate, we want to pay our own way. We want God to use our money for more important things. Yet the Old Testament reveals that God considers a communal celebration of grace extremely important. It gives us a wonderful reminder that the tithe did not function in a purely legalistic fashion. The great King of Israel is so benevolent and gracious that he returns a portion of the tithe to his people to allow them to celebrate his goodness and mighty acts of deliverance. God pays for the ministry of his church out of his own pocket! So immense is God's grace. Those who comprehend this gracious giving of God "learn to revere the LORD . . . always" (14:23).

JUSTICE AND THE OLD TESTAMENT ECONOMY

Some Christians believe that the entire subject of Old Testament giving can be confined to a discussion of the tithe. But that's just where Old Testament giving began, not where it ended. God did not want the Israelites to think that after giving God a cut, they could keep the other 90 percent for themselves. The tithe was only one expression of God's call to practice justice and mercy within the Israelite community.

A key text in understanding this vision of life in God's kingdom is Exodus 22:21-24: "Do not mistreat an alien or oppress him, for you were aliens in Egypt. Do not take advantage of a widow or an orphan. If you do and they cry out to me, I will surely hear their cry. My anger will be aroused." The prescribed economic system was based upon Israel's experience of God's saving work. Israel knew the injustice of Egyptian slavery. The Israelites' Egyptian taskmasters had shown them no mercy. But God delivered Israel. Now Israel must demonstrate to the economically disadvantaged the same justice and mercy it received.

Seen in that light, the little-known rules and regulations of the law of Moses begin to make sense. We have a tendency to dismiss much of that legislation as meaningless to New Testament believers. After all, our modern society cannot possibly practice a Year of Jubilee without destroying our carefully balanced economic structures. And it would make no sense to prohibit farmers from reaping the corners of their fields. But when we look at this ancient legislation in the light of agrarian culture, we see that these laws intend to construct a community where justice and mercy intersect.

NO-INTEREST LOANS

Consider God's expectations concerning the harvest:

> *When you are harvesting in your field and you overlook a sheaf, do not go back to get it. Leave it for the alien, the fatherless and widow, so that the LORD your God may bless you in all the work of your hands. When you beat the olives from your trees, do not go over the branches a second time. Leave what remains for the alien, the fatherless, and the widow. When you harvest the grapes in your vineyard, do not go over the vines again. Leave what remains for the alien, the fatherless and the widow. Remember that you were slaves in Egypt. That is why I command you to do this.*

> *—Deuteronomy 24:19-22*

Why does God require such beneficence from Jewish farmers? The Lord reminds them of their own need for grace. Their kindness to others reminds them of the infinite kindness they received. It's fascinating to ponder whether our own benevolent giving today awakens in us any sense of solidarity with the people to whom we minister. Benevolent giving is simply one beggar sharing God's unmerited provisions with another beggar.

God also made pronouncements concerning usury: "If you lend money to my people, to the poor among you, you shall not deal with them as a creditor; you shall not exact interest from them" (Ex. 22:25, NRSV). To make sense out of this command, we must recognize the dynamics of ancient rural culture. The economy of Israel was primarily agricultural. The reason to seek a loan was survival, not just financial return. "Loans in Israel were not commercial but charitable, granted not to enable a trader to set up or expand a business but to tide a peasant over a period of poverty" (Getz, *A Biblical Theology of Material Possessions*, p. 264). So when Israelites sought loans, they really needed charitable gifts. Money borrowed at interest would only reduce them to deeper poverty. Concern for justice and mercy color God's attitude toward usury.

This concern invites us to reconsider how we handle money. Should we charge interest on a loan we make to help someone pay a staggering hospital bill or to meet life's bare necessities?

SABBATH YEARS AND JUBILEE

The Old Testament's concern for economic structures that alleviate the burdens of the oppressed continues in the Sabbath cycle of years:

> *Every seventh year you must grant a remission of debts. And this is the manner of the remission: every creditor must remit the claim that is*

held against a neighbor, not exacting it against a neighbor who is a member of the community, because the LORD's remission has been proclaimed.

—*Deuteronomy 15:1-2, NRSV*

This provision for canceling debt did not intend to make life easy for bad borrowers. It was a recognition of the tendency of every community to polarize financially. As the saying goes, "The rich get richer and the poor get poorer." In *Starting Even* Robert Haveman reports that in the U.S. today nearly 70 percent of the wealth is concentrated in the hands of the richest 10 percent of the population. Federal Reserve figures indicate that in 1988, 54 percent of United States' citizens had no net assets (Smith, *The World's Wasted Wealth*, p. 2). The Old Testament vision of society, however, includes a big middle class in which average citizens can feed their families and relax in comfort under the shade of their own fig trees.

Grace toward the debtor is enlarged even more in the keeping of the Year of Jubilee (Lev. 25:11-13). Israel celebrates the Year of Jubilee in connection with the seventh Sabbath year. All property is returned to its original owners. In an agrarian culture wealth is primarily related to land. That's still true today. After the Second World War many Dutch farmers immigrated to America in search of farmland. The scarcity of land in the Netherlands forced many farmers to become sojourners in another country. The Year of Jubilee kept native Israelites from becoming dispossessed in their own land and experiencing a similar fate.

This practice of returning land was a remarkable expression of Israel's stewardly office. Its basis is theological as well as practical. The Year of Jubilee serves as a recognition that Israel is only a tenant living on land that God owns: "The land must not be sold permanently, because the land is mine and you are but aliens and my tenants" (Lev. 25:23).

NEW WINESKINS

The Old Testament tells us a great deal about giving. Justice and mercy must lace our culture today just as they pervaded Israelite society three thousand years ago. Of course, we need to take into account that necessary structures to achieve them are different today. The poor of Chicago cannot be helped by a farmer in Wisconsin who leaves apples unpicked in the orchard. A sweeping law against charging interest hardly seems appropriate in an economy in which borrowed money is used for capital expansion. But issues of justice, mercy, and compassion are as pressing for us today as they were for God's Old Testament people. Our challenge is to devise the appropriate wineskins from which we can pour the wine of justice and compassion into our society today.

The Israelites did not do well in fulfilling God's command to them. Tragically we have no evidence that they ever kept the Year of Jubilee. The prophets repeatedly denounce them for ignoring God's commands regarding economic justice. Malachi bemoans the way Israel robs God of his tithe (Mal. 3:8). But he also indicts Israel for oppressing the widows and the fatherless and depriving aliens of justice (Mal. 3:5). Israel's failures show clear signs of the need for God's law to be written upon hearts of flesh rather than tablets of stone.

God issued the basic principles. God's commands were clear. But faithful stewardship and abundant giving awaited a new era of grace. We shall focus on that in the next chapter.

SESSION SUGGESTIONS
FOR THE LEADER

Scripture Reading: Deuteronomy 24:10-22

Ask a volunteer to read the passage. Even though we were not slaves in Egypt, has God given us good reason to show the same amount of generosity to the needy? Discuss this question briefly.

Quotable Quotes

Invite someone to read each quote and reflect on its meaning. Entertain reactions from the group.

> *Our assessment of Israel's giving patterns is woefully off the mark if we think that Israel gave in order to receive divine love. For Israel giving was supposed to be a sign of gratitude, just as it is for us.*

> *More is involved in bringing homage to God than merely presenting an offering. The attitude of the heart is as important as the gift presented.*

> *I wonder whether our complaints might be a subtle sign that we have difficulty receiving graciously from a giving God. When it comes time to celebrate, we want to pay our own way. We want God to use our money for more important things. Yet the Old Testament reveals that God considers a communal celebration of grace extremely important.*

> *Why does God require such beneficence from Jewish farmers? The Lord reminds them of their own need for grace. Their kindness to others reminds them of the infinite kindness they received. It's fascinating to ponder whether our own benevolent giving today awakens in us any sense of solidarity with the people to whom we minister.*

> *Israel's failures show clear signs of the need for God's law to be written upon hearts of flesh rather than tablets of stone.*

Implications and Applications

If these questions help to structure your discussion, terrific. If not, devise your own. Give priority to questions raised by participants.

1. What are the three uses to which Israel had to put the Old Testament tithes? Any parallels today? Check out, for example, 1 Timothy 5:17-18 to get you started—your pastor will appreciate it!

2. What was the purpose of loans in Israelite society? In our society is it legitimate to distinguish between business loans and charitable

loans? What is God's will revealed in the Old Testament laws concerning loans? How does God's will apply to the loans we make?

3. What was God's will in proclaiming a Year of Jubilee? Any lasting significance for us today?

4. How can justice and mercy lace our culture today in a society where the economic structures are so different?

5. Are tithes and offerings still valid concepts for today? How literally should we take them?

Closing Worship

Because the giving that pleases God emerges from a thankful heart, let celebration of God's grace and goodness be the focus of your closing worship. List instances where God has richly blessed you communally and personally. Join in some robust songs of praise. In closing prayer admit your poverty, also in giving. Ask that God's Spirit will make you rich in giving instead. Pray the same thing for the congregation you lead. Conclude your prayer with thanks for God's wondrous gift of salvation and the many concrete gifts it involves.

CHAPTER 5

GIVING: NEW TESTAMENT REALITIES

The Spirit of the Lord is upon me,
because he has anointed me
to bring good news to the poor.
He has sent me to proclaim release to the captives
and recovery of sight to the blind,
to let the oppressed go free,
to proclaim the year of the Lord's favor.

—*Luke 4:18-19, NRSV*

Jesus chooses these words for his first sermon. He attends synagogue in Nazareth, his hometown. As a son of the synagogue Jesus is invited to read Scripture. He chooses a text from Isaiah that is familiar to his readers. It's not the text itself but the way he begins his sermon that stuns the crowd: "Today this scripture is fulfilled in your hearing" (Luke 4:21).

This motif of fulfillment offers us the key to understanding Jesus' ministry. Christ is an enigma apart from the Old Testament. His ministry makes sense only when we understand that it fulfills Old Testament promise. In chapter 4 we saw that the Exodus became the foundation for the economic patterns of God's Old Testament people. Now God's incarnate Son makes possible a new Exodus, which represents the ultimate expression of God's grace. It constitutes the central saving event that shapes the economics of God's New Testament people.

NEW ECONOMICS

God's grace still forms the foundation for the lifestyle of God's people, just as it did in the Old Testament. The in-breaking of God's kingdom leaves no part of living untouched. It pours the Spirit of God upon every earthly reality. Not just formal religion, but family, labor, and government are all transformed by the divine power of Christ. Life in God's kingdom is continually centered in Christ's redeeming grace.

That all-embracing salvation penetrates our billfolds, purses, and checkbooks too. The text Jesus quotes at the beginning of his public ministry alludes to economic matters. Christ comes "to proclaim the year of the Lord's favor" (Luke 4:19). That's the Year of Jubilee mentioned in Leviticus 25, the Sabbath of Sabbaths, when all debts are canceled and slaves set free. Isaiah catalogs the diversity of economically disadvantaged people who need to be freed: the poor, the captive, and the oppressed. Now what Isaiah foreshadowed in the Year of Jubilee is coming to fulfillment in Christ's ministry. An era dawns that embodies all that it's supposed to be.

The implications of this text extend far beyond economic issues. The fulfillment of Jubilee will mean peace, love, and joy beyond anything the world has seen. But we should not spiritualize the text so that the economic and financial implications disappear. Virgil Voogt, a pastor of a Mennonite church that pioneers economic restructuring, notes,

> *Jesus proclaimed a more profound and comprehensive Jubilee, one in which all sins (i.e., all debts) could be canceled, all bondage—psychological and spiritual as well as economic—could be broken, and all captives could go free. Yet there is no indication that he meant to leave the economic meaning behind. Indeed, Jesus initiated a kind of open-ended era of economic Jubilee, one facet of the larger messianic announcement of the "acceptable year of the Lord."*

—Voogt, Treasure in Heaven, pp. 75-76

So the New Testament sheds new light on our financial stewardship. It does not abolish Old Testament principles but takes them up into the new kingdom realities that have dawned in the ministry of Christ. Let's look at the kingdom wine that bursts the economic wineskins of the Old Testament age.

THE TITHE AND THE NEW TESTAMENT

Consider the most commonly asked question about our giving. Guilt-ridden, middle-class Christians, haunted by their anemic giving patterns, inquire fearfully, "Does the New Testament teach that we still have to tithe?" Those who pose the question tend to have reason for their discomfort. They have likely read Malachi and discovered his stern words against Israel's neglect of the tithe (Mal. 3:8-10). They wince when they fill out their income tax returns and discover how little they give to charity. If they were Old Testament believers, Malachi would be speaking directly to them. The Pharisees definitely shared that concern. They were so certain that neglect of the tithe had contributed to the exile that they tithed even the herbs in their gardens. No wonder many serious Christians want to know what their attitude toward tithing should be!

Christ's attitude toward the tithing practices of the Pharisees can be seen in Matthew 23:23: "Woe to you, teachers of the law and Pharisees, you hypocrites! You give a tenth of your spices—mint, dill and cummin. But you have neglected the more important matters of the law—justice, mercy and faithfulness." To us the approach of the Pharisees seems overly scrupulous. I doubt that many Christians today would think of tithing the tomatoes in their garden, let alone the dill weed. Yet Jesus does not condemn these religious leaders for carrying the tithe to such ridiculous extremes. He commends their precision. But he presses on to explore the critical issue: the way in which they keep the law while they deny its intent. They can tithe and still ignore the mercy and justice it means to cultivate. Speaking of the way Pharisees devote their resources to God in order to escape supporting their aged parents, Jesus concludes, "Thus you nullify the word of God by your tradition that you have handed down" (Mark 7:13).

What a shocking discovery! Even the tithe has a dark side. It can legalistically limit our participation in the generosity that marks life in God's kingdom. The Year of Jubilee is here today. Yet we can fail to participate in the free and joyful giving that God intends it to bring.

THE LAW OF LOVE

Against this background we can answer the question we asked earlier: "Do I have to tithe today?" When we catch the vision of what God has done in Christ, the question becomes moot. We live in an age marked by such divine self-giving that it led God's Son to hell and back. That reality makes the law of love more than enough to motivate us towards grateful giving. Can God's people still measure their gratitude in percentages? Do we need pocket calculators to decide whether we've given our fair share this month? The tithe is an old wineskin that the kingdom age has burst asunder.

Other New Testament writings echo that conclusion. The epistles are completely silent on the tithe. The New Testament nowhere reaffirms the tithe as the giving standard for the church. In fact, Paul rejects any externally imposed rule of giving when he reminds his churches to give as each member purposes in his or her heart.

He spells out the reason in Galatians 4. The Old Testament age was one of spiritual immaturity (Gal. 4:1-3), in which God's children needed the law to serve as their tutor. The present kingdom age is an age of maturity. Grown-up sons and daughters of God, led by the Spirit, are freed from the law's constraints (Gal. 3:25). So we must be careful not to impose a tithe on our congregations as if we are dealing with Old Testament believers.

Some churches distinguish tithes from offerings. Tithes are brought into God's storehouse—the local congregation. Offerings go beyond the tithe and can be given to causes of choice. This kind of logic, however, still imposes Old Testament categories on New Testament believers.

ABIDING PRINCIPLES

We need to add an important caution. God did not impose the Old Testament tithe in an arbitrary, capricious fashion. The tithe expresses certain abiding principles.

A tenth was a significant portion of a person's income, especially in a subsistence culture. Thus God clearly expects people to give a significant portion of their resources. Secondly, the amount of the tithe increased with income. The greater the financial blessing, the greater the gift we should return to the Lord. Paul reiterates that principle when he stipulates that one's giving should be "in keeping with [one's] income" (1 Cor. 16:2). And finally, if God expected the spiritual children in the Old Testament to give a tenth, will God expect any less from spiritual adults? Getz rightly observes, "Though the tithe laws were never perpetrated in Christianity as they were in the Old Testament, they serve as models to Christians for regular and systematic giving" (*Real Prosperity*, p. 45). That is precisely what we find in the early church.

THE BENEVOLENCE OF THE EARLY CHURCH

Empowered by God's Word and Spirit, the life of the early church demonstrates economic realities never seen before in the history of the world. It never dawns on early church members to measure out a tenth of dill and cumin in order to meet God's expectations. They give lavishly, extravagantly, even rashly—a bold example of a church that seriously attempts to pattern its life after the self-giving of its Savior (Phil. 2:4-5).

Descriptions in Acts 2:44-45 and 4:32-35 of the way the early church holds goods in common have led to much debate. Some argue that the descriptions found here are purely fictional, merely attempts to describe a utopian fellowship that never existed (Gonzalez, *Faith and Wealth*, p. 80). But there are good arguments to demonstrate that these are not fabrications. Could such boldfaced lies circulate so soon after the church was born? Other ancient documents provide collaborating evidence that the descriptions in the book of Acts are fact (Bassler, *God and Mammon*, p. 118).

But we can still ask how far that commonality of goods actually went. Some contend that the sharing of goods was total and absolute.

They maintain that the Christian community embraced its own version of communism in which it rejected on principle the concept of private property. In their judgment this radical rejection of private ownership contributed significantly to the abject poverty we find in the early church and made it necessary for Gentile Christians to launch the church's first fund drive for their Jewish counterparts (Gonzalez, p. 81).

But this interpretation misses the point. "They would sell their possessions and goods and distribute the proceeds to all, as any had need." These words from Acts 2:45 make clear that selling property was not carried out by all believers at the same time. The church in Jerusalem never rejected the right of private property. The selling of goods was an ongoing phenomenon prompted by continuing need within the early church. As Peter clearly indicated to Ananias, no one was forced to sell property (Acts 5:4). Its surrender was a voluntary act of Christian compassion.

THE DAWN OF JUBILEE

So what happened in the early church? We can understand it best as a remarkable expression of what the dawning of the messianic Jubilee brings. Christ begins to establish that Jubilee through his death and resurrection. In Luke 4 we discover that the proclamation of "the year of the Lord's favor" (v. 19) means "good news to the poor" (v. 18). We need to read Acts 2:45 in that light: the followers of Jesus "[sold] their possessions and goods [and] gave anyone as he had need." Acts 4:34 adds, "There were no needy persons among them. For from time to time those who owned lands or houses sold them, brought the money from the sales and put it at the apostles' feet." Clearly the words of Isaiah concerning the Year of Jubilee were being fulfilled in the lives of those who embraced the gospel.

This idea may leave us uncomfortable. If the principle of private property was not abandoned by the early church, how can Acts 2:44 say that "all the believers were together and had everything in common"? We find the key in Acts 4:32: "All the believers were one in heart and mind. No one claimed any of his possessions was his own." Voogt observes, "Individuals still possessed things, yet they had all things in common. Their attitudes toward economic things were so changed that individual ownership did not define individual use. Everything that they owned was available for common use. It didn't matter who possessed it" (p. 80).

What the early church discovered was the radical nature of stewardship. God is the owner of all things. We are God's trusted stewards, called to keep faithful oversight of what our Creator has placed in our hands. The early church recognized that this faithfulness demanded first and foremost a concern for the needs of the poor. The economic stewardship that accompanies the gospel demonstrates the justice and mercy that God intends for the Year of Jubilee. As God's people in the Old Testament should already have understood, possession and ownership are two radically different things. I own nothing although I possess a great deal. But what I possess is always at the disposal of God's kingdom.

SHARING GOODS

The term *koinonia* carries this implication. The word means more than just a sharing of warm feelings among friends. It's used in ancient times to describe a business partnership where two individuals share common business property (Gonzalez, p. 83). Christian *koinonia* includes more than spiritual sharing. It includes material sharing as well. Understood in this way, the practice of the early church remains relevant. It sets the pattern that Paul describes in 2 Corinthians:

> *I do not mean that there should be relief for others and pressure on you, but it is a question of fair balance between your present abundance and their need, so that their abundance may be for your need, in order that there may be a fair balance. As it is written,*
> > *The one who had much did not have too much,*
> > *and the one who had little did not have too little.*

> —*2 Corinthians 8:13-15, NRSV*

What this means in practice becomes clear in a remarkable case study that Paul offers us on the matter of giving. Today we often call it "The Great Collection."

A CASE FOR GIVING CHRISTIANS

Every time we pass the plate we hope to realize a great collection. But when Paul thinks of the Great Collection, he has in mind the offering we read about in 2 Corinthians 8 and 9. Paul's concern in that passage goes deeper than a sensitivity to human need that spurs him to pass the hat. For Paul the collection plate in Corinth harbored deep theological significance.

We need to review some history to understand why. The Jerusalem Council (Acts 15, Gal. 2) forms the backdrop to the Great Collection. There Paul meets with the pillars of the Hebrew-speaking church. Real differences emerge between these Christian leaders. The key issue is whether Gentiles need to become Jews to enter the kingdom of God. Paul knows that the integrity of the gospel hangs in the balance. Eventually the council affirms that Gentiles stand shoulder to shoulder with Jews in the Church of Christ. Paul's gospel is vindicated. The leaders in Jerusalem do ask Paul to discourage his congregations from practices that cause deep offense to their fellow Christians in Jerusalem. And they ask one more thing: "Remember the poor." Paul assures the church at Galatia that this is one request he eagerly embraces (Gal. 2:10).

Who are these poor people? They are not just the poor in general but those in the church of Jerusalem. That's evident from the energy Paul invests over the course of eight years to gather money from his Gentile churches for the Jerusalem church (Bassler, p. 89). At times the collection seems to consume Paul's thoughts. We wonder why as we read this passage. The needs of Jerusalem may be extreme, but poverty is certainly not unique to Palestine. The Macedonian church itself undergoes a "severe trial" (2 Cor. 8:2). Yet Paul commends this impoverished congregation for its generous giving. Then why does Paul show such preoccupation with the ingathering of gifts for Jerusalem?

THE REAL MEANING OF THE COLLECTION

New Testament scholar Keith Nickle, in his book *The Collection*, argues persuasively that Paul attaches three layers of meaning to this collection. First, the collection is a matter of sheer benevolence—an act of Christian love and charity. The Christian's concern for those in poverty is a reflection of Christ's own concern. Jesus has already taught the need for benevolence when he reminds his followers that what they do for even the least among people, they do for him (Matt. 25:40).

Secondly, Paul finds great significance in the collection as a symbol of the solidarity between the two branches of the infant church. The deep, theological significance of the collection comes to expression when we see the interplay between Gentile and Jew in Romans 15:25-27. Paul stresses that Jew and Gentile are involved in a unique gift exchange. Spiritual gifts have flowed from Jew to Gentile. Now material gifts flow from Gentile to Jew. In that way they both affirm the solidarity of the church. As Bassler notes, by accepting the gift, the Jewish Christians "tacitly acknowledge the validity of the Gentile mission" (p. 94).

The fear that this acknowledgment will not come about plagues Paul. He requests prayers that his "service in Jerusalem may be acceptable to the saints there" (Rom. 15:31). Paul knows that the Jewish church could reject these gifts because it does not want to affirm the unity that they symbolize. The Jerusalem church is well aware that financial sharing is a sign of the fellowship (*koinonia*) of the saints. By receiving this gift, it affirms that Christian *koinonia* extends beyond Jewish circles to Gentiles. Paul actually uses the term *koinonia* in Romans 15 to describe the collection itself.

A third reason why Paul find this collection so significant is that it signals the beginning of the end time, the close of this present age. The collection proclaims a Jew-Gentile unity that none of Paul's contemporaries expected to see in this present age. But the Jewish Scriptures prophesied a day when the Gentiles would come to Israel: "Nations will come to your light, and kings to the brightness of your dawn" (Isa. 60:3).

Does Paul see the collection for Jerusalem as a fulfillment of this prophecy? Does this explain the size of the Gentile entourage that accompanies Paul to Jerusalem? The large number of Gentiles who accompany Paul (Acts 20:4; 1 Cor. 16:3; 2 Cor. 8:18-23) provide secure passage for this financial gift. But it seems that security measures alone could hardly justify the expense of transporting such a large number of people. Paul probably saw their presence fulfilling Old Testament prophecy: the peoples of all nations are now coming to Jerusalem to bring their gifts to Israel.

The purposes of the Great Collection still address our motivation for giving today. We give for purely benevolent purposes. But the financial gifts that flow among churches of differing ethnic, racial, and social groups continue to show that God is breaking down dividing walls of hostility and building us all into a single people. We've become accustomed to giving for causes worldwide. We collect money to help the hungry in Kenya. We send support for missionaries in Nigeria and the Philippines. We provide what's needed—both in time and money—for neighborhood programs that minister to people from a variety of races and cultures. Yet we so easily forget how amazing our behavior is. By our giving we declare that national boundaries no longer box in the church of Christ. Our gifts are a powerful sign that our ultimate allegiance is to a kingdom that knows no earthly boundaries.

HOW WE SHOULD GIVE

From Paul we learn much about the motive for kingdom giving. We also discover something about the spirit in which we should give. A crisis in stewardship prompts Paul's remarks. The collection at Corinth has stalled. Disruptions from false teachers have destroyed enthusiasm for the project. We can only understand Paul's insistence that the collection resume if we grasp the theological significance he attaches to it. But the advice he gives to the Corinthians on how they should proceed is downright practical. From it we learn at least four things about Christian giving.

- *Our giving should be systematic.* Paul instructs the Corinthians to give weekly on the Lord's Day (1 Cor. 16:2). That's when the church celebrates her new life in Christ. First-day giving expresses gratitude to the self-giving Savior. It becomes part of the regular rhythm of Christian worship equal to the Old Testament firstfruits giving.

- *Our giving should be proportional.* The Corinthians must give in keeping with their income (16:2). Christian giving is not a tax levied on every Christian across the board. As was true in the Old Testament, those who have more should give more.

- *Our giving should be without compulsion.* Paul does not demand a predetermined percentage such as a tithe. He makes clear that his guidelines are not commands (2 Cor. 8:8). Each believer should give as he purposes "in his heart to give, not reluctantly or under compulsion, for God loves a cheerful giver" (2 Cor. 9:7). Paul's reticence to regulate does not mean he considers generosity inconsequential. He notes that giving "test[s] the sincerity of [our] love" (2 Cor. 8:8).

- *We should give expectantly.* Generous giving is a sign of a sincere faith. Those who sow generously expect to reap generously (2 Cor. 9:6). Paul promises: "You will be made rich in every way so that you can be generous on every occasion, and through us your generosity will result in thanksgiving to God" (2 Cor. 9:11).

The promise Paul makes in 2 Corinthians 9:11 leaves fertile ground for what is sometimes called the "prosperity gospel": if giving begets riches, then give generously in order to get rich! While we should reject such a health-and-wealth interpretation, we must be careful not to move to the opposite extreme either. It is unduly narrow to say that the blessings that accrue from giving are only spiritual. But the prosperity gospel seems to ignore the fact that Paul also says in 2 Corinthians 9:8 that God gives us all we need but not everything we crave.

CALLED TO FIRSTFRUIT GIVING

The economic life of the early church expresses concretely the messianic Year of Jubilee that Christ ushers in by his death and resurrection. When the apostolic age draws to a close, the church continues to give expression to that same commitment to bring good news to the economically disadvantaged. A Christian manual of instruction written toward the end of the first century called *The Didache* declares, "Do not hesitate to give, and do not grumble when giving, for you will know who is the glorious giver of your reward. Do not turn away from those who are in need but share all things in common."

Will the church today heed the ancient admonition? Only if we faithfully teach and encourage our members in firstfruit giving. We cannot assume that church members will automatically develop faithfulness to God's call. We, as church leaders, need to cultivate economic stewardship.

MISSION MONEY

The gospels reveal two preaching missions: that of the twelve (Luke 9:1-5; Mark 6:6-11; Matt. 10:5-15) and that of the seventy-two (Luke 10:1-20). While the parallel accounts in the gospels differ slightly, all agree on the general tenor of these missions. Jesus sends his disciples out, exemplifying radical poverty (no money, no provisions). He places careful strictures on their freedom to solicit support (accept the first offer of hospitality; do not change lodging places).

Jesus gives these instructions to provide living examples of the radical demands for faith and obedience to which the gospel message they bring calls people. "In the way they conducted their mission, the disciples were to exemplify a trust in God so profound that the most basic preparations for a journey were unnecessary" (Bassler, p. 43).

Paul's comments on mission support indicate that Jesus does not intend to make this a normative pattern that we must follow woodenly in every missionary situation. But we can derive at least two principles these preaching missions reveal about the way the church should raise mission money.

- The radical trust in God these missionaries show remains a perennial expectation for the church. When fund-raising techniques replace our trust in God, then our church has lost its bearings.

- Our mission endeavors should recognize the power to transform the lives of those to whom the gospel comes. "The missionaries' message would evoke in some villagers a positive response that would result in an offer of food and shelter" (Bassler, p. 44). Ongoing dependence on the sending mission is unhealthy and denies the power of the Spirit of God to provide for the expansion of the gospel.

The missions of the twelve and seventy-two are of short duration, set within a special context of salvation history. Jesus implies that the instructions he gives them will be superseded by others. At the Last Supper he commands, "But now if you have a purse, take it, and also a bag" (Luke 22:36).

NEW DIRECTIONS

Paul also signals a new direction in mission support. His thinking on the subject is complex, and his practice sometimes seems less than consistent. A closer examination reveals that Paul's principles do not change. What does change is the ministerial setting in which he applies them.

The first principle Paul affirms is the right of those who preach the gospel to receive financial support through it. As an apostle Paul insists on this right in Corinth (1 Cor. 9:18). From his letter to the Philippians we can infer that he accepts financial support from them (Phil. 4:15-16). He describes this support as a *koinonia*, a partnership in the gospel. Thus the same dynamic working in Paul's ministry is at work in the early church. When we share financial resources to meet needs, we enhance the spiritual fellowship of the church.

Paul qualifies this right with a second principle: the proclamation of the gospel must be effective. Christians should voluntarily surrender those liberties that create obstacles to the gospel. In the same way Paul renounces his right to financial support if monetary issues threaten the effectiveness of his preaching (1 Cor. 8-9).

Paul's application of this principle at Corinth leads to unexpected complications. The "super-apostles" who follow Paul treat his refusal to accept support as a sign of the inferiority of his ministry (2 Cor. 11:12-13). Paul's defense of his action carries his argument beyond what is found in his first letter to the Corinthians. His action is a voluntary renunciation of privilege for the sake of the gospel. It also demonstrates that the nature of the gospel calls us to service, not privilege; weakness, not worldly success (2 Cor. 11:27-30).

Paul's principles still guide our church today. Our Lord not only permits but also expects us to give financial support to the gospel ministry. This situation establishes *koinonia* between ministers and local churches. At the same time, those who receive financial support must monitor any negative fallout that results from it. When financial support becomes a stumbling block to the gospel, they should decline it.

HANGING ON LOOSELY

Our Christian community lives in the expectation of the *parousia*, of Christ's coming again. From that perspective our material possessions do not have ultimate importance. They are not evil, but they are not enduring either. Paul notes, "The time is short. From now on ... those who use the things of the world [should live] as if not engrossed in them. For this world in its present form is passing away" (1 Cor. 7:29-31). Christians live with a loose grip on their goods. Their ultimate possession is to be possessed by the Lord Jesus Christ.

SESSION SUGGESTIONS
FOR THE LEADER

Scripture Reading: Acts 2:42-47

Ask a volunteer to read the passage aloud or do so yourself. Briefly discuss what led these Christians to hold onto their goods with such a loose grip. What does that mean for us today?

Quotable Quotes

Invite someone to read each quote and reflect on it. Then discuss it together.

> God's incarnate Son makes possible a new Exodus, which represents the ultimate expression of God's grace. It constitutes the central saving event that shapes the economics of God's New Testament people.

> Even the tithe has a dark side. It can legalistically limit our participation in the generosity that marks life in God's kingdom. . . . The tithe is an old wineskin that the kingdom age has burst asunder.

> The church in Jerusalem never rejected the right of private property. The selling of goods was an ongoing phenomenon prompted by continuing need within the early church.

> What the early church discovered was the radical nature of stewardship. God is the owner of all things. We are God's trusted stewards, called to keep faithful oversight of what our Creator has placed in our hands. The early church recognized that this faithfulness demanded first and foremost a concern for the needs of the poor. . . . Possession and ownership are two radically different things. I own nothing although I possess a great deal. But what I possess is always at the disposal of God's kingdom.

> Paul instructs the Corinthians to give weekly on the Lord's Day (1 Cor. 16:2). That's when the church celebrates her new life in Christ. First-day giving expresses gratitude to the self-giving Savior. It becomes part of the regular rhythm of Christian worship equal to the Old Testament first-fruits giving.

> Christians live with a loose grip on their goods. Their ultimate possession is to be possessed by the Lord Jesus Christ.

Implications and Applications

Here are some possible questions to toss into the discussion brew.

1. Do we, like the Pharisees, still "keep the law but deny its intent"? How?

2. Read Luke 4:18-19. What does it mean that Jesus brought in the Year of Jubilee? What implications does that have for us?

3. How does the law of love motivate and guide our giving in this New Testament era?

4. Heerspink tells us that the Old Testament tithe has been superseded by the coming of the Messiah. But it still yields some abiding principles to guide our giving. What are they? How should they function in our congregations?

5. What can Paul's Great Collection teach us about our giving?

6. Time to lighten up a little. Share together some memorable stories or experiences that influenced or shaped your attitudes towards giving. (As leader you may need to "prime the pump" on this one.)

Closing Worship

The most profound influence upon our giving is the advent of Jesus Christ, who has already ushered in "the year of the Lord's favor" (Luke 4:19) and whose return we eagerly anticipate. In your worship focus on him. In songs and prayers celebrate this greatest gift of God that prompts us, in turn, to gratefully give ourselves and everything we have back to our Lord.

CHAPTER 6

BRINGING STEWARDSHIP TO THE PULPIT

At least once a year preachers would prefer *not* to be recognized on the pulpit. During their annual stewardship messages they would prefer to hand out written copies of their sermons for the people to read while the preachers themselves hide behind the pulpit.

Perhaps not every pastor is forced to preach a stewardship message once a year. Only 40 percent of churchgoers claim to have heard a sermon on stewardship themes in the past twelve months (*God and Mammon in America*, Wuthnow, p. 141). That's in spite of the wealth of biblical material on the subject. Pastors using the common lectionary find that few passages related to financial concerns have made their way into the yearly cycle of readings. We shouldn't be surprised. Few pulpit themes are as difficult to treat. I can relate to that intimidated pastor—ready to go into the service with a bag over his head!

Why is preaching stewardship such hard work? This is an important question for preachers who make the sermons, elders who supervise them, and deacons who must help God's people apply them. While this chapter focuses specifically on pastors, the rest of the leadership team should listen in as well. As we have seen, proclaiming stewardship should be a combined effort.

OBSTACLES TO PREACHING STEWARDSHIP

Preaching about stewardship is tough because few people in the pew think that such sermons really address their personal needs. Parishioners seldom encourage such preaching for their own benefit. They always see these sermons as being important for someone else, for those who give less to the church budget than they do. During a stewardship message the congregation is alive with busy listeners, spotting others in the pew who need to hear what the preacher just said. If they could get away with it, they would nudge their neighbors in the ribs at pertinent points. As a result the sermon on stewardship suffers the miserable fate of being perceived to apply to no one personally.

Another obstacle is that sermons on stewardship seem to bristle with hidden motives. While we speak glibly of giving to the Lord, we all know that it's tough to channel our money directly to the courts of heaven.

One well-known story tells of three pastors who are comparing the way they separate their wages from general church receipts. One reports that he draws a circle on the floor, throws the money in the air, and claims for himself all that falls outside the circle. Another reports that he does it a better way: he also draws a circle but claims for himself all that falls inside the circle. A third reports that he has improved even on that approach. He throws the money up into the air and says: "Lord, take for yourself, all you want." What falls back to earth he considers his wage.

GOD'S RECEIVING HANDS

I have news for those pastors. No one gives directly to God. All the money we give to the Lord goes to ministry done in the Lord's name. That's as it should be this side of eternity. But that fact creates tension for pastors who want to teach stewardship. The congregation often senses a vested interest in the message. When preachers exhort the congregation to practice stewardship, what the congregation often hears is this: "Give more to maintain the financial solvency of this church."

As a pastor of a congregation I'm often visited by wonderful people representing Christian organizations. They drop by on a regular basis to update me on the great things happening in their ministries. I believe them. But I am well aware that they are in my office for more than just to prod me to add their ministry to my prayer list. They're there because their organization needs my congregation's financial support. So I'm always a bit on guard for vested interests in these visits.

When I preach from the pulpit about money, my congregation raises its guard as well. Worshipers fear that the message is motivated more by the church's need to receive than by their need to give. It makes preaching stewardship a tough job.

THE POOR LEADING THE POOR

A third reason why preachers shy away from preaching about stewardship may be a personal one. We ourselves may be poor financial stewards. Just because we are ordained to the ministry of the Word and Sacraments doesn't mean that we are ready to set an example of careful financial management and sacrificial giving. Like others in their congregations, pastors can be poor money managers and bad loan risks.

It's easy for us to rationalize bad stewardship and giving: if we'd gone into other careers, we could have made a lot more money. Consequently, we pretend that our career commitment to the pastorate constitutes our financial contribution to the kingdom. Or we blame our lack of stewardship on the fact that the church didn't come through on a well-deserved raise. So we give ourselves that raise by decreasing our contribution to the general fund.

When we play these games, sermons on financial stewardship unveil our own hypocrisy. How can we ask the congregation to give sacrificially if we have never done so ourselves? How can we ask the congregation to live a modest lifestyle when we burn with desire to buy the latest electronic toy? Effective preaching isn't just something that happens in the worship service. Effective preaching begins with the integrity of the minister.

Pastors need not stand at the very pinnacle of the stewardship mountain before they preach a stewardship sermon. They wrestle right alongside their parishioners to bring the financial side of life into conformity with kingdom ideals. Preaching stewardship doesn't demand perfection on their part. But it does demand that they embark on that road themselves before they ask the congregation to make the journey to committed stewardship.

Martin Luther once said that three conversions are necessary for one to become a Christian: the conversion of the heart, the hand, and the purse. It may be necessary for us as pastors to undergo that third conversion before we are spiritually prepared to preach stewardship from the pulpit.

GUIDELINES FOR THE STEWARDSHIP SERMON

If preaching on stewardship is so tough, why should we do it at all? Is it merely the great cost of keeping today's churches afloat that makes it necessary? Hardly! The need to preach about stewardship is not primarily related to the pile of church bills on the treasurer's desk. It's related to the congregation's need to hear the whole counsel of God. That counsel takes us right into the arena of financial giving.

Thomas Jefferson once took scissors and clipped out the parts of Scripture he found offensive. He rejected references to the miraculous and abridged his Bible to bring it into conformity with his own way of thinking. Not too many of us would actually take scissors to the Bible. Yet we mentally cut out parts of it that raise our discomfort levels. Many of us excise not the mention of miracles, but of money. That means we do a lot of cutting. More than two thousand verses in Scripture mention stewardship matters. Even to serious Bible students it still comes as a shock that nearly half of Jesus' parables deal with money and wealth.

Any pastor attempting to preach the full counsel of God cannot escape the subject either. So here's some guidance for preaching on the unavoidable topic of stewardship:

- *Don't be embarrassed by the topic.* Often we introduce a sermon on stewardship by apologizing for bringing up the subject. Don't apologize! Don't be ashamed to preach about it. If you are uncomfortable with your subject, the congregation will be too. Don't trivialize your message by begging the congregation's indulgence.

- *Don't go where Scripture does not go.* The Bible has much to say about financial stewardship. Simply preach what it says. In money matters we must avoid the temptation to ride our personal hobbyhorses and to expound our own economic theories. Let's not befuddle the congregation by mixing the gospel message with our own idiosyncratic speculations. There is enough material on stewardship in Scripture to keep preaching fresh for a lifetime.

- *Approach financial stewardship with healthy humility.* Admit that you're preaching to yourself as much as to the congregation. It's tough to practice what we preach and often we, too, need a word from the Lord about our finances. Avoid setting yourself up as a paragon of economic virtue. I willingly admit I don't have all the answers. But I invite my congregation to struggle with me so that we can help each other bring our financial lives into greater conformity with the Word of God.

- *Make sure your stewardship preaching is bathed in grace.* Few preaching topics tempt us as strongly to return to legalistic prescriptions. We cram our stewardship sermons with "oughts." We compare our comfortable lifestyles with that of poor people on skid row. Guilt becomes our favorite motivator for improving the congregation's stewardship.

We should learn some lessons from a master pulpiteer. When it's time to talk about stewardship, the apostle Paul weaves grace and giving together. He closes 1 Corinthians 15 by celebrating the incredible victory over death we possess in Christ. Grace has robbed death of its venom. Victory is ours in Christ. Because later editors have put a chapter division here, we tend to stop reading. But consider Paul's next words: "Now about the collection for God's people" (16:1). Paul sees the link between Christ's open grave and our open billfolds. Grace compels our giving. In our giving we follow the example of Jesus Christ, who emptied himself for us even though he was rich (2 Cor. 8:9).

Because of the pressure to keep the general fund solvent, we easily drive a wedge between God's grace and our gifts. But if we do not give out of grace, then we give out of guilt. Guilt makes us regard stewardship as a bane instead of a blessing.

WIDENING OUR VISION

Another way that pastors can energize sermons on stewardship is to broaden their vision. J. Michael Walker, stewardship consultant with the Presbyterian Church (U.S.A.), points out that churches with a Stewardship Week on their calendars soon begin to think of stewardship as just another season of the church year, like Advent or Lent. That approach, he maintains, allows congregations to conclude that stewardship is only a matter of concern around the time when we're struggling to balance the church budget. We need to enlarge that understanding.

Stewardship is certainly about treasure. But it's also about time, talents, and trees. It involves what we give away. However, stewardship also deals with managing what we keep. It's an appropriate sermon topic any time of year. Money is as much a part of our daily lives in January as it is during the autumn budgeting process. Stewardship season runs year-round. So it should be a regular theme from the pulpit. Pastors must demonstrate to the congregation that they preach about financial stewardship because it constitutes an important part of obedience to Jesus Christ. It isn't a concern just to get the church out of the end-of-the-year budget crunch.

MEETING A REAL NEED

As pastors we often shy away from the subject of stewardship because we don't see how it meshes with the needs of our people. We see how it may impact the needs of the local church to start a new community ministry. We see how it meets the needs of the denomination to keep joint ministry projects afloat. We don't see, however, how giving connects with the needs of our individual members. But it does, in at least two ways.

First, we need a cause greater than ourselves for which to live. Without it we wander aimlessly through life. Our investment in what is truly important to us is more than just financial. But money remains one of the critical ways we invest. We identify with our dollars. They represent hours of effort and energy. When we give them, we affirm our need to live for something beyond ourselves.

Second, we who experience the grace of the Lord need to express our thanks. That happens in various ways. The Heidelberg Catechism lists prayer as the chief avenue of thanksgiving. But our giving remains an important way as well. The unspeakable gift of Christ our Lord prompts our giving.

We preach on financial stewardship because our churches *need to receive*, but more importantly, because *we need to give*. Haddon Robinson, professor of homiletics at Gordon-Conwell Seminary, observes, "When I preach on money with these two needs in mind, it frees me. No longer am I laying on people an unwanted burden. Instead, I am offering people a thirst-quenching opportunity to involve themselves in something that outlasts them, and to express their gratitude to God" ("Preaching on Money: When You've Gone Meddlin'," p. 4).

A HEALTHY MIX

I've discovered one other way to improve my preaching on stewardship. I combine it with other teaching methods. This book is written to accompany an adult educational course entitled *Firstfruits: Managing the Master's Money* (Lillian Grissen, Barnabas Foundation, 1992). When I field-tested it with my congregation, I combined it with a series of sermons. Evaluations later indicated that this "one-two" punch was greatly appreciated. The Reformed Church in America offers a similar stewardship program entitled, "Consecrating Stewards."

Sermons raise questions as well as answer them. As stewardship sermons instruct, they also raise issues in the minds of parishioners. How *do* I teach my children a proper way of handling money? What *is* a proper lifestyle for a disciple of Christ in today's world? We need an open forum to explore such questions. A course or a discussion period after the sermon will allow a congregation's members to think these issues through.

SILENCE IN THE PULPIT

It's commonly observed that churches are always talking about money. I wonder if that's so. I suspect that we *think* our church talks more about money than it actually does. This I know—few churches talk much about stewardship. In our preaching we shouldn't just talk about money. We should preach about stewardship. Our people are looking for guidance in addressing money matters from a Christian perspective. Stewardship is at the heart of the perspective they need.

The sermon guides in Appendix A are included to help you get started. They give a sampling of how stewardship messages can be developed. These guides are from a series of messages that were originally correlated with the *Firstfruits* stewardship course that's available through CRC Publications, the RCA Distribution Center, and the Barnabas Foundation. Messages like these can be given in conjunction with such a course, but they can also stand on their own.

A word of encouragement to those who hesitate to take the first step: will your preaching make a difference? Believe it! A recent study shows that those who hear biblical messages on finances are more likely to give generously to their churches (Wuthnow, p. 143). But we don't really need a sociological study to tell us that. God told us long ago:

> *As the rain and the snow*
> *   come down from heaven,*
> *and do not return to it*
> *   without watering the earth*
> *and making it bud and flourish,*
> *   so that it yields seed for the sower*
> *   and bread for the eater,*
> *so is my word that goes out from my mouth:*
> *It will not return to me empty,*
> *but will accomplish what I desire.*
>
> *—Isaiah 55:10-11*

SESSION SUGGESTIONS
FOR THE LEADER

Scripture Reading: 1 Timothy 6:1-19

Ask someone to read the passage for the group. Paul twice tells Timothy what to command of the rich (vv. 17,18). Isn't that asking Timothy to come on too strong? How bold should we be when leading God's people into stewardship?

Quotable Quotes

Read and discuss the following quotes:

> *Worshipers fear that my message is motivated more by the church's need to receive then by their need to give. It makes preaching stewardship a tough job.*

> *Martin Luther once said that three conversions are necessary for one to become a Christian: the conversion of the heart, the hand, and the purse. It may be necessary for us as pastors to undergo that third conversion before we are spiritually prepared to preach stewardship from the pulpit.*

> *The need to preach about stewardship is not primarily related to the pile of church bills on the treasurer's desk. It's related to the congregation's need to hear the whole counsel of God. That counsel takes us right into the arena of financial giving.*

> *Because of the pressure to keep the general fund solvent, we easily drive a wedge between God's grace and our gifts. But if we do not give out of grace, then we give out of guilt. Guilt makes us regard stewardship as a bane instead of a blessing.*

> *Stewardship is certainly about treasure. But it's also about time, talents, and trees. It involves what we give away. However, stewardship also deals with managing what we keep. It's an appropriate sermon topic any time of year.*

Implications and Applications

1. What makes it so hard for us to preach or talk to people about their giving?

2. Participants will have to go gently but firmly on the following question. We don't want to be critical, but as church leaders we must be willing to help and support each other in providing good leadership in the area of stewardship. Heerspink gives some concrete advice to

pastors on how to preach stewardship messages. Which parts of that advice would you particularly commend to your pastor? What advice would you add to Heerspink's?

3. Read 1 Corinthians 15:56-16:2. What's the link between Christ's open grave and our open billfolds?

4. In what ways does preaching on finances really connect with the needs of the congregation? How can you as council demonstrate support for your pastor's preaching by making this clear to the congregation?

5. Heerspink states that preaching on stewardship was greatly enhanced by combining it with other teaching methods. What might be some that you can use in your church? Will you?

Closing Worship

This is an excellent opportunity to pray for one another as church leaders. Confess before God the ways in which you have failed each other as a leadership team called to promote stewardship. Ask God specifically for the things your fellow council members need to fulfil that task: courage, patience, kindness, the right things to say, an appropriate opportunity. Give thanks for what you have already accomplished and for the joyful, faithful giving of so many of the saints in your church. Conclude your prayer with praise to the Lord to whom we belong and who, through Christ, belongs to us.

CHAPTER 7

WHAT MAKES GIVERS TICK

W eek after week the bulletin of Old First Church reports a nagging $17,000 deficit in the general fund. The pastor mentions it from the pulpit. The treasurer makes a special announcement that an extra $170 from each of the one hundred households will erase the deficit. But despite their impassioned appeals the flow of red ink continues. "Let's face it," mutters an elder at the monthly council meeting, "our people just don't have the income to support this kind of a church budget."

Oddly enough, Old First collects $3,000 in a single offering in response to a special denominational appeal for hurricane victims. When the bulletin carries a request for contributions to send five young people to Haiti to build an orphanage, five anonymous donors underwrite the entire cost of the plane tickets. And when a local task force looks for money to organize a neighborhood teen center, it's Old First Church that the organizers hail as the most generous congregation in the community. The elders just don't get it. The general fund is running in the red, but the people have plenty of money to give to everything else.

What happened at Old First is happening in hundreds of congregations across the country. What's going on?

FREE TO GIVE

We labor under the delusion that a little education is all we need to put congregational stewardship back on the right track. A bit of training, a few stewardship messages, and all will be well. But teaching stewardship to our parishioners is only half the battle. Why? Because once our congregations better understand it and commit themselves to practice more generous giving, they still need to decide which causes to support.

Some people argue that all the money should go to the local church. The "storehouse-tithe" concept, espoused by some traditional congregations, considers the local church the modern-day equivalent of the storehouse mentioned in Malachi 3. In their view church members must bring a full 10 percent (tithe) to their congregation before they bring offerings to other causes.

Although such an interpretation is institutionally welcome, it's exegetically suspect. It confuses church and kingdom. It also takes an approach to giving that most parishioners find unacceptably authoritarian. Increasingly, church members want to exercise more discretion about their giving. They look for better accountability from organizations they fund. Few church members today will respond to a wooden mandate to give 10 percent of their income to their church's general fund. They will continue to make personal decisions about the direction of their giving. But how do they decide?

To answer that question, let's consider what motivates Christians to give as they do. What kinds of factors come into play as Joe and Jane Pewsitter decide where to channel their giving?

MY JOURNEY BEGINS

Let me share a bit of my own journey toward understanding stewardship better. The churches I've served have tended to operate financially like Old First: after adopting the budget, the council hoped against hope that the money would materialize in the collection plate. Sometimes the church made budget. Most years it didn't. Tension concerning the balance in the general fund built through the lean summer months and typically boiled over at the September council meeting. Council would schedule catch-up offerings for the general fund. They were usually ineffective because passing the plate a second time during the same Sunday for the same fund didn't make much sense to the people in the bench.

My thinking about stewardship changed when I took up my present pastorate, and as a council we began to focus on the church's mission instead of on stewardship itself. Before I assumed my duties at the Cottonwood Church, council indicated to me that there was a pressing need to sharpen the church's vision. My first job would be to launch a long-range planning committee that would take a hard look at what the church was about and where it was going.

As the committee answered the question of Cottonwood's identity—how the church could better become "who we were"—it became evident that committee members were singing the same refrain again and again: "But we don't have enough money! Sure we need more staffing, but how are we going to pay for it? Sure we need more ministry to the community, but where are we going to get the bucks? Sure we need more classrooms—even an enlarged sanctuary—but where are we going to find the megadollars to make all that possible?"

Although we know that nothing may stand in the way of what God calls us to do, money often becomes the tail that wags the dog. Tacking an extra thousand dollars on the budget becomes a real hurdle when the general fund is already running in the red.

DROPPING THE OLD REFRAIN

The committee's discussions gave me a feeling of deja vu. I had encountered this same talk in my two previous churches. I had heard the same refrain: "We'll do it when we have the money." I thought that response was prompted by size. My previous churches weren't big enough to do more than maintenance ministry. Coming to a larger church, I didn't expect to hear it again. But Cottonwood Church was twice as big as the church I'd just left, and it still sang the same tune. It became clear to me that size is no guarantee that financial resources will automatically materialize for an expanding mission. Bodies don't translate automatically into bucks. *Every* church tends to see itself living on the financial edge!

To their credit the members of Cottonwood's long-range planning committee refused to be put off by dollar amounts. The church's rallying cry became, "Bring them to Christ! Bring them to Cottonwood! We're going to make plans that will enlarge our mission to this community. We will do what it takes to make room for new members."

That approach meant that we needed to take another look at the entire matter of stewardship. We discovered that money and mission sustain a very tight relationship. Cottonwood Church couldn't do mission without money. But Cottonwood members weren't going to give money without a ministry vision big enough to shake the dollars from their pockets. We had to face reality. One reason the general fund lagged was because we hadn't established or communicated a vision big enough to motivate the congregation.

MONEY AND MISSION

George Salstrand, in *The Story of Stewardship in the United States of America*, notes this relationship between giving and vision. Tracing the history of giving in America, he shows that it rises during those periods of history when the church takes seriously its calling to be a leaven in society and a light to the world. Salstrand concludes, "Missions and stewardship are partners. One cannot be missionary-minded without thinking of life and possessions in terms of stewardship" (p. 25).

This observation seems so obvious. Yet most churches ignore it. They assume that mission follows money, that when more money comes into the church's coffers, then it's time to expand the church's mission. But the reverse is true: money follows mission. Where the work of the Lord advances, money tends to follow in its wake because giving is part of our broader stewardship: the stewardship of the gospel of Jesus Christ, our greatest treasure. Believers tend to give where they see exciting things happening for Christ's sake. No church can expect to grow in giving if it is not growing in mission. A church that engages merely in organizational maintenance can expect giving to plateau and then diminish.

MOTIVATORS

The issue of motivation means that the church's leaders must take a close look at the way they try to encourage giving. The average council rarely makes a sufficiently clear appeal to the congregation's mission. Church consultant Kennon Callahan provides us with a helpful analysis. He identifies five major motivational resources for giving among church members:

- *compassion*: the desire to translate love into caring
- *community*: the desire to build relationships with others
- *challenge*: the desire to achieve a proposed goal
- *reasonability*: the desire to act because careful analysis indicates the course of action makes good sense
- *commitment*: the desire to respond out of loyalty, obligation, and commitment

—Callahan, Twelve Keys to an Effective
Church: The Leader's Guide, p. 76-83

These motivating forces exist in all of us. All five can appropriately stimulate Christian behavior. Yet few of us have an equal mix of them. Callahan argues that two of the five tend to predominate in the average person. And the two that predominate in the leaders are not always the same two that predominate in the membership.

Typically *challenge* and *commitment* form the language council members speak: "If this congregation were more committed, we'd have all the money we need for the budget. What we need to do is challenge our people more—lay it on the line! We have to tell them to 'walk their talk.' " Most leaders are very familiar with that lingo, which casts the matter of giving primarily into those motivational categories.

The problem is that these two motivators don't connect with most church members. On the grassroots level *compassion* and *community* tend to be more powerful factors for motivating giving. Consider again Old First Church. A challenge to give more to the general fund falls on deaf ears.

But members eagerly respond to the opportunity to aid disaster victims (compassion) and contribute funds for a new teen ministry center (community).

MAKING THE CONNECTION

A little reflection helps us to understand what is happening. Compassion and community relate directly to the mission of the church. Whether it's an effort to reach inner-city kids or to start a new church on the other side of town, such mission efforts spell **care** and **fellowship** in bold letters. Typical church members find these the most fitting causes to which they can channel their gratitude to God and their desire to share the gospel of Christ.

Commitment and challenge are second-tier motivators. We find them predominantly among those who experience the care and compassion of a church over the course of years. That's why they resonate more easily with church leaders than with younger members. Elders who have been touched by thirty years of ministry at Old First Church don't need reminders of how this church gave them care and community during hard times. They're deeply committed to the church that stood by them when they were unemployed or grieving. A call to commitment says to them, "Keep the ministry of this church rolling!" The prior care and community of the church has built up the commitment they need to respond to the church's challenge for greater giving.

In my first parish the new parsonage was funded through the estate of someone who had never been a member of the congregation. The father of this generous donor had been pastor of this little rural church well into his eighties. His wealthy son always remembered the kindness shown to his father. The congregation might easily have put the elderly minister out to pasture, but it didn't. The compassion that the son had seen in that little congregation gave rise to a commitment that lasted a lifetime. Care, compassion, and community build a foundation for commitment and challenge.

Consequently, we should remember that many members still need to experience the care and community of the church if they are going to respond to the second-tier motivators of commitment and challenge. And we must make them aware of our church's significant ministries that warrant their solid financial support. Community and compassion are such powerful motivators because they take us into the realm of people. Most of us give so that we may touch other people with the love of Christ.

PUTTING PRINCIPLE INTO PRACTICE

Here are three practical suggestions to help your council connect with the congregation when it comes to giving:

- *Take a close look at the mission statement of your church.* Is it still a meaningful statement of your congregation's communal calling? If you don't have a mission statement, initiate a process to draft one. An excellent resource to help you do so is *Focus,* available from CRC Publications. Make sure your mission statement reflects biblical principles as well as the field where God has planted your congregation. Exegete your community setting as well as Scripture. Your church has its own, unique calling from God to communal ministry, so your mission statement should include a biblical definition of the church and the angularities of your specific parish setting. Many congregational mission statements have a bland flavor because they are too generic. They may be biblical, but they lack the ability to inspire the church's mission. They are so ill-defined that they allow the church to swing in many directions. The result is that they provide no useful guidance and leave the church hanging.

- *Communicate your mission statement to the congregation.* How familiar is your congregation with your mission statement? Has anyone read it lately? Can you even locate it? At Cottonwood the mission statement provides the framework for the first worship service after Labor Day, marking the beginning of our fall church year. The sermon focuses on the church's mission. The congregation reaffirms aspects of the mission statement in the liturgy. Banners in the sanctuary celebrate the statement's key components. We hang them in the sanctuary several times a year to remind ourselves of our identity and calling as a congregation. We incorporate aspects of the mission statement into the design of the church bulletin. The mission statement forms a vital part of the information packet we distribute to new and prospective members. We want to keep the vision before the congregation.

- *Follow up with careful planning.* Even if your members know your mission statement by heart, that doesn't mean anything unless it actually shapes the life of your congregation. What kind of organizational structure is in place to assure that the mission statement guides your short- and long-range planning? Is your congregation pursuing goals that emerge out of this document?

- *Let your congregation in on the link between your mission statement and your actual mission.* Consider adding a *Moment for Ministries* to your worship service on a weekly or monthly basis. When a missionary visits your church, give a mission report. Offer a ministries report in which someone from your own congregation relates mission happenings within your church. Ask your pastor to interview someone involved in a specific ministry, then remember it in a special way in congregational prayer. Over a period of time worshipers will discover congregational ministries they never knew existed.

A COMMUNAL CONCERN

These suggestions are a good beginning, but we need to do more. For people today money has become such a private aspect of their lives. Giving is a very personal matter. As the television screen flashes a financial appeal in response to some international crisis, spouses might nudge each other to suggest sending money. But the approach is haphazard. So much for thoughtful, planned giving! Giving is ad hoc and very much "our own business." It's no wonder that many churches feel compelled to adopt a hands-off approach to money. They fear that dollar talk will alienate the membership.

But that attitude isn't acceptable if we see the church God's way. In Bonhoeffer's words, we should view the church as "Christ existing as community." That's a radical vision. The church is not a voluntary organization of religiously-oriented people but a divinely created reality that manifests Christ's own life by the power of God's Spirit. As Christians are united to God, they are also bound together with unbreakable cords. This means that our stewardship is personal, but it cannot be individualistic. Financial stewardship is one of the key ways in which the church concretely expresses its unity. As church leaders we carry the awesome responsibility of nurturing our congregation's corporate stewardship.

Doing that remains one of our greatest challenges. Wuthnow points to the basic tension in our society that complicates any encouragement to give. In the minds of many Americans asking for money is "unspiritual." When they spend too much time on fund-raising, organizations turn off potential givers. One person in fourteen thinks he or she would give more generously if his or her church emphasized money more. But one in three said that he or she would give less! Wuthnow concludes, "It restores public confidence in the orderliness of its cultural distinctions to believe, for example, that Mother Teresa of Calcutta is unconcerned about money or to know that generations of preachers, from Cotton Mather to John Wesley to Billy Sunday, died with virtually no money to their names" (p. 233).

We should not take Wuthnow's observation to mean that we can't talk about money in church. As we have seen, faith and finances intersect. But his observation warns us that we need to think through what will be the best way to cultivate our congregation's giving. A simple plea for more money often doesn't work very well. Placing a deacon in front of the congregation to deliver the yearly "Woe is us, we are financially undone" speech doesn't solve the church's money problems. If it did, you wouldn't be reading this book!

In the next chapters we will get down to specifics about ways we as church leaders can encourage serious financial stewardship within our congregations. We must approach the matter honestly, refusing to sell out the biblical perspectives we have examined. We must also resist the temptation to engage in manipulation and gimmicks. We will discover that we can do much and do it with integrity. Given some time, a church can take important steps to encourage the congregation to take stewardship seriously.

SESSION SUGGESTIONS
FOR THE LEADER

Scripture Reading: 2 Corinthians 9:6-15

After reading this passage together, reread verses 14-15. What's the gift mentioned in verse 15? How will those whose "hearts . . . go out to you" know that the Corinthians really have this gift?

Quotable Quotes

Read and discuss the following. For a change of pace allow a volunteer to choose the quote she or he wants to talk about.

> *Teaching stewardship to our parishioners is only half the battle. Why? Because once our congregations better understand it and commit themselves to practice more generous giving, they still need to decide which causes to support.*

> *Although we know that nothing may stand in the way of what God calls us to do, money often becomes the tail that wags the dog.*

> *Money follows mission. Where the work of the Lord advances, money tends to follow in its wake because giving is part of our broader stewardship: the stewardship of the gospel of Jesus Christ, our greatest treasure.*

> *On the grassroots level compassion and community tend to be more powerful factors for motivating giving. . . . Compassion and community relate directly to the mission of the church. . . . Typical church members find these the most fitting causes to which they can channel their gratitude to God and their desire to share the gospel of Christ.*

> *Our stewardship is personal, but it cannot be individualistic. Financial stewardship is one of the key ways the church concretely expresses its unity. As church leaders we carry the awesome responsibility of nurturing our congregation's corporate stewardship.*

Implications and Applications

1. Heerspink observes that parishioners want the freedom to exercise more personal discretion over their giving. How can we make that possible and still meet the financial obligations of our congregations and denomination?

2. Heerspink cites five motivators for giving listed by Callahan. Which of these primarily motivate your council members? Which primarily motivate your congregation? Your teens? Your seniors?

3. How can a well-conceived, well-communicated mission statement influence giving in your church? Do you have one? Do your congregation members know what it says without looking it up? If you don't have one, what can and will you do about this situation?

4. How are you putting your mission into practice in your church? How do you figure out where God wants you to go next?

5. How might we turn God's people off in broaching the subject of giving? How can we inspire them instead?

Closing Worship

When we look at the magnitude of the mission God has given us, we may easily become discouraged and feel unequal to the task of leading God's people to fulfill it. In prayer lay your feelings of inadequacy before God. Seek the revitalizing power of God's Spirit. Commit yourselves to do the little day-to-day things we can do and trust God to do the big ones. Conclude your prayer with a song that emphasizes again the revitalizing strength and power of God.

CHAPTER 8

STEWARDSHIP AND THE LEADERSHIP TEAM

F red and John share a cup of coffee after the morning service. Talk turns to their involvements in the congregation. "Say," John asks, "what happened to that stewardship committee you headed up when you were in council?"

Fred shrugs. "It fell apart shortly after I retired as deacon."

"What happened?"

"Well, I guess I was the only one really excited about promoting stewardship in this church. The other committee members only served in order to do me a favor. When I retired as chairman, the committee dissolved within six months."

Unfortunately, that conversation has its counterpart in dozens of other churches. Often we hear it from a well-meaning council member who offers to do something to promote better stewardship. Sometimes we hear it from a couple of members of the congregation who approach council and offer to teach a class or provide financial counseling. The council accepts their efforts in a spirit of "what can it hurt?" Nothing significant comes of their efforts because stewardship remains the pet project of a handful of parishioners. It drifts in a congregational backwater. For financial stewardship to be mainstreamed, the whole leadership of the church must adopt stewardship as a high priority.

At Cottonwood Church we discovered that stewardship involves a number of leadership dimensions. As the pastor I led initial efforts with the full support of the council as a whole. That support for stewardship was unusual. Many pastors find themselves lone voices in that area. Their councils abandon them to twist slowly in the wind should their stewardship initiatives go awry. I won't be numbered among them. My council backed me strongly from the beginning.

But we at Cottonwood still discovered that something was missing: we lacked a committee structure to give council guidance. Over the next several years we looked first to the deacons, then to the finance committee, then to the executive committee to provide that leadership. In the end we did what we should have done three years before: we appointed a standing stewardship committee to lead the way. This structure provided us with three leadership groups—pastor, council, and stewardship committee. The Bible says, "A cord of three strands is not easily broken" (Eccles. 4:12). That's especially true when it comes to stewardship efforts.

THE PASTOR LEADS THE WAY

It pains me to write the words that head this section because, as a pastor, I am weary of being told that the senior pastor is the linchpin who holds together every program. Everything from social action to evangelistic outreach to small group life is heaped on my plate. Without my spiritual leadership all will be in vain. Yet how far can I stretch myself before I start to come apart at the seams?

Nevertheless, when it comes to stewardship, the pastor *does* need to lead the way. In a study conducted among congregations whose giving was double the national average, the number-one reason members gave generously was strong pastoral leadership (Grimm, *Generous People*, p. 151). Unless the pastor is committed to cultivating stewardship in general and financial stewardship in particular, little will happen in the congregation. This fact carries at least four implications for pastors.

1. *Pastors need to take a second look at stewardship in their own lives.* Many pastors convince themselves that simply entering the ministry resolves their own personal stewardship. They believe they have already sacrificed a great deal for God's kingdom. Pastors work long hours. Because their salaries are seldom comparable to other professionals with similar years of training, some pastors convince themselves that these sacrifices absolve them from any serious financial giving to Christ's kingdom. But the fact that a pastor has been appointed steward of the mysteries of that kingdom does not mean that all personal stewardship issues have been resolved. Many useful tools are available to help pastors with their personal stewardship. One that I've found especially useful is Ron Blue's *Master Your Money*, available through the RCA Distribution Center, the Barnabas Foundation, and CRC Publications.

2. *Pastors need to tell their own stewardship stories.* I recall talking to a fellow pastor about financial problems in his congregation. The church was running behind in budgeted giving. The deacons had hit upon a new strategy to address the problem. Because the pastor was one of the better givers in the congregation even though his salary was much less than that of many church members, they intended to announce that the pastor was among the top five contributors to the church.

The council hoped that the pastor's example would shame many in the congregation into giving more.

There isn't a more inappropriate approach to encourage giving. Telling their stories doesn't mean that pastors announce in the bulletin their weekly contributions to the general fund. Nor does it mean that they engage in a pious triumphalism that sets them apart as philanthropic paragons. It means instead that they willingly share something of their own journey towards more faithful stewardship. Congregations will discover that pastors face the same financial pressures and cope with the same temptations that sidetrack grateful giving as they do. Pastors should lead by example as well as precept.

3. *Pastors should utilize their role as the congregation's theologian-in-residence.* Pastors don't always realize the influence they wield in the congregation through their role as educator. If a pastor doesn't preach or teach that stewardship is a key component of the Christian lifestyle, members of a congregation aren't going to put it high on their list of priorities. The pulpit shapes the vision of the church. Good preaching not only instructs, it inspires. The pulpit is still a key for setting a church's stewardship agenda.

4. *Pastors should provide intentional leadership.* Few people in church know more about stewardship than the pastor. Many ministers may protest that they are not good at numbers. Their churches may be filled with bankers, bookkeepers, and CPAs. No doubt there will be number crunchers who know more about balancing the books than the pastor does. But few are likely to know more about stewardship. Even if the council appoints a stewardship committee, the pastor must still retain the responsibility of providing wise guidance on stewardship matters. Because financial stewardship interlocks with the overall vision and mission of the church, the stewardship committee needs the pastor's support. It needs to know that, as it steers the church into uncharted waters, the pastor will not jump ship when a question or criticism arises concerning a new stewardship effort. Eugene Grimm argues,

> *The pastor's leadership can help people catch the vision of going to new regions where they "have never gone before" and look forward to the trip. Stewardship apart from mission is as uninviting as stagnant water. When mission and spiritual growth is the focus, stewardship becomes a stream flowing in the desert. The pastor, as planning facilitator, adds the pragmatic wheels to the biblical engine.*

> —Grimm, p. 44

CRITICAL SUPPORT

Early in my ministry a colleague gave me a desk card that reads: *If it is to be, it is up to me.* I soon learned that statement needs serious qualification, especially when it comes to making changes in the life of an average congregation. Pastors are not ecclesiastical dictators. For a church to move forward with integrity, the council needs to exercise joint leadership with the pastor.

That's particularly true of financial stewardship. Kennon Callahan points out that many churches hamstring their own financial stewardship because their leaders lament, scold, complain, and whine about the state of the congregation's finances. In communicating with the congregation about money, the leaders become harassing parents, scolding their children about fiscal irresponsibility. Callahan points out that such behavior has an assured result: "The more scolding is done in your congregation, the more anger will be raised. The more whining is done, the more unhealthy pity will be generated. Generosity and giving will be diminished, not increased, by such negative approaches" (*Giving and Stewardship in an Effective Church*, p. 11).

Stewardship begins with leaders who understand that the congregation of which they are a part is enlivened and empowered by the Holy Spirit. Christ is working through the congregation. His kingdom will not fail. Their church is part of a winning cause—God's. But there are specific things that council members should do to give leadership in the area of stewardship.

1. *They will need to make a serious study of stewardship issues.* A council that leads will take time to discover that congregational stewardship is much more than just passing the offering plate during Sunday worship. Council members will understand that it's just as important to have a working knowledge of financial stewardship as it is to familiarize themselves with the church order and effective pastoral care. Consequently, they must take the time to study the biblical principles and the practical structures that advance financial responsibility in the church. Several excellent resources are available to equip council members. *Firstfruits: Managing the Master's Money* is an outstanding introduction to stewardship, which council can study before offering to the congregation as a whole. It's available through CRC Publications, the Barnabas Foundation, and the RCA Distribution Center. Earl Miller's *Consecrating Stewards with a Focus on a Consecration Sunday* also provides an excellent resource. It specifically concentrates on the need of the giver to give, rather than the congregation's need to receive financial support. It emphasizes proportionate giving and challenges members to increase the percentage

of what they give to God as grateful stewards. It's available through the RCA Distribution Center. Kennon Callahan's *Giving and Steward-ship in an Effective Church* offers a fine exploration of the organization-al implications of financial stewardship in the local church. Council could explore these resources at its yearly retreat. These studies could also become the basis for ongoing education throughout the year.

2. *Council members will need to reassess their personal stewardship.* What holds true for pastors holds true for church leaders as well. If council mem-bers are not willing to take a hard look at the way they handle mon-ey, they cannot lead others toward a healthy approach to finances. As leaders we cannot challenge our congregations to more faithful stew-ardship without first challenging ourselves. The most powerful tool a council has is example.

3. *A council that takes stewardship seriously recommits itself to taking leadership.* Many stewardship efforts shipwreck on the rocks of fear and uncer-tainty. Stewardship is one of the most exhilarating areas of ministry, but it is also one of the most intimidating. Many churches work hard to try to produce an elephant, but they only bring forth a mouse. When the time comes—after all the study and assessment—to ask what concretely should change, the leaders' courage fails. The status quo is maintained with only slight modification. Many churches do tune-ups even though a total engine overhaul is needed. When new approaches to stewardship are on the table, the question that needs to be asked is whether council members have enough courage to exer-cise the authority Christ has entrusted to them and lead the church forward in faithful obedience.

CONSTRUCTING THE GAME PLAN

If the council is responsible for stewardship, why is it necessary to form a stewardship committee? A church council needs to do so for the same reason that it can be dedicated to Christian instruction but needs an education committee to put wheels on the church-education program.

In my experience councils typically try to toss the matter of steward-ship into the lap of an existing group, such as the finance committee. But a finance committee is better equipped to deal with administering funds than with leading the congregation to provide them.

In some churches the diaconate is charged with the job of guiding stewardship. That makes sense because stewardship is part of the dia-conal mandate. But most diaconates are simply too large to function ef-fectively as a committee of the whole. Financial stewardship will advance in the average church only if a committee is appointed that gives its full attention to it.

MAKEUP OF THE STEWARDSHIP COMMITTEE

Who should serve on a stewardship committee? Obviously, the best people possible. They are not necessarily the church's financial wizards, but they should be comfortable talking dollars and cents. They should be equally comfortable talking obedience, discipleship, and sacrifice. The following are four specific recommendations regarding the membership of a stewardship committee.

- *Good stewards make good committee members.* Committee members should set an example of what stewardship is all about. This does not mean that only big givers should be appointed. Stewardship is more the sacrificial attitude that accompanies the gift than the size of the gift itself.

- *Good committee members have good people skills.* Stewardship consists more of raising the level of discipleship than of raising the level of giving. Members should have solid communication skills. They should also relate well to others and be comfortable talking to them about stewardship.

- *Appointees should have the respect of the congregation.* Often new stewardship initiatives call the congregation to stretch and establish new comfort zones. A committee comprised of people who have the respect of the congregation makes such efforts easier. Council members and parishioners alike will try something new when the proposal comes from leaders who have earned their trust. A good committee can give the council and congregation the strength to go where they have never gone before.

- *The committee should reflect the breadth of the congregation.* Deacon and elder representation is important, but the committee should include both young and old, men and women. Diverse membership will not only enhance the work of the committee but also convince the congregation that financial stewardship is a discipleship issue for everyone.

THE COMMITTEE'S MANDATE

No committee can function without a mandate. Many committees have been appointed only to be left wondering what it is they are supposed to do. The stewardship committee should focus on four areas of responsibility:

- educating the congregation regarding a biblical understanding of stewardship
- advising the council on procedures and policies that will encourage the stewardship of the entire congregation

- organizing a stewardship campaign that will encourage each church member to make a solid financial commitment
- communicating with the congregation on a regular basis regarding the church's giving and practice of stewardship

To function effectively, the stewardship committee will need to work closely with other committees and groups in the church. Stewardship education demands that the committee work with the church's educational ministries. A stewardship campaign will bring the committee in close working relationship with the finance and long-range planning committees. Communicating with the congregation means close association with the church's diaconate. In many respects the stewardship committee provides an umbrella under which the united efforts of the congregation take place. It should always do so in close cooperation with the leadership as a whole.

Now that we have explored the role that church leaders can take in cultivating congregational stewardship, we will move on in chapter 9 to take a look at the church budget and the role it can play in motivating the congregation to fulfil its mission as God's stewards.

SESSION SUGGESTIONS
FOR THE LEADER

Scripture Reading: Acts 6:1-7

Although the seven who were chosen fulfill many responsibilities that we entrust to our deacons, they did other things as well (see 8:4-5). What we find here is a differentiation of the tasks that are essential to the life of Christ's church. While the tasks may be parceled out according to gifts, the work itself remains fundamentally unified. What is the work that we all seek to accomplish as ordained and unordained leaders in the church? Do we remain equally responsible for the task of fellow leaders? Does the team concept apply? Discuss this briefly.

Quotable Quotes

> For financial stewardship to be mainstreamed, the whole leadership of the church must adopt stewardship as a high priority.

> The pulpit shapes the vision of the church. Good preaching not only instructs, it inspires. The pulpit is still a key for setting a church's stewardship agenda.

> Pastors are not ecclesiastical dictators. For a church to move forward with integrity, the council needs to exercise joint leadership with the pastor.

> What holds true for pastors holds true for church leaders as well. If council members are not willing to take a hard look at the way they handle money, they cannot lead others toward a healthy approach to finances. As leaders we cannot challenge our congregations to more faithful stewardship without first challenging ourselves. The most powerful tool a council has is example.

> In many respects the stewardship committee provides an umbrella under which the united efforts of the congregation take place. It should always do so in close cooperation with the leadership as a whole.

Implications and Applications

1. What are the advantages of mandating a stewardship committee as a separate entity? What's the downside, if any?

2. Should the pastor lead the way towards responsible stewardship in your church? If you disagree, then who should? If you agree, does your pastor feel the same way?

3. What should pastors do in giving leadership in this area? What should elders do? Deacons? Stewardship committees? How will you be sure everyone knows their job and does it?

4. Heerspink thinks that scolding is not a good motivator towards better congregational giving. Do you agree? What's a better approach? How will you implement it?

5. Does your church need only a tune-up or a whole engine overhaul when it comes to the practice of stewardship? How will you tackle it?

6. What qualities should the people have that you appoint to the stewardship committee? What should the committee's mandate look like?

Closing Worship

Thank God for the many ways in which your congregation and its leadership have been blessed with a vision of faithful giving. Ask forgiveness for opportunities unmet. Pray for inspiration and vision that continue to transform your congregation into "living sacrifices, holy and pleasing to God—[which] is [our] spiritual act of worship" (Rom. 12:1). Seek our Lord's guidance as you plan future initiatives.

CHAPTER 9

MISSION BUDGETS: BEYOND LINE ITEMS

I t's hard to understand," Jay remarked. "Our last congregational meeting drew less than 10 percent of our voting membership. Ever since we scheduled a spring congregational meeting to elect elders and deacons and a fall meeting to approve the budget, fewer and fewer people attend the autumn meeting."

"Must be everyone is totally satisfied with the finances of the church," answered Mark.

"Maybe, but folks sure complain if there is something they don't like about the way the money is spent. No matter how hard we plead with them, however, attendance just keeps dwindling."

There may be many reasons why attendance decreases at such fall meetings. But instead of just challenging the absentee members or pleading with them for a greater commitment to attend, Jay and his fellow church leaders may want to ask whether the agenda they have prepared for the meeting has sufficient drawing power. Does it have enough significance to motivate the average parishioner to attend?

THE BUDGETING PROCESS: AN UNFORTUNATE HISTORY

In many churches the council's financial goal when preparing the budget is to do next year what was done this year—as cheaply as possible. Most churches operate with a line-item budget, listing the various categories of expenditures. Keeping in mind the inflation rate for the previous year, the finance committee will work through last year's line items and try valiantly to keep increases to no more than a cost-of-living adjustment. The goal is to hold the line on increases and bring to the congregation a budget that increases no more than the inflation rate.

Such an approach operates with several presuppositions. First, it assumes that stewardship is really just another word for thrift. Good stewardship becomes a euphemism for frugality. The implicit principle operating in financial planning becomes "come weal or come woe, our status is quo." But the church's corporate stewardship must consist of neither profligate spending nor penny-pinching stinginess. Congregational stewardship calls us to a careful, obedient use of our resources to accomplish the work God has entrusted to us.

A second assumption the traditional approach makes is that the congregation is already giving "to the max." This means that any budget increase must be held to the percentage of increase parishioners have likely experienced in their own income levels. The truth is, however, that few parishioners are giving anything near their full capability. The Ecumenical Center for Stewardship Studies reports that the average percentage of giving to local congregations in four major U.S. denominations ranged from 1.2 percent to 2.9 percent of members' income (Hoge and Griffin, *Research on Factors Influencing Giving to Religious Bodies*). Most churches have only begun to grow in their financial stewardship.

The traditional approach guarantees a ho-hum budget so vanilla-flavored that it generates no enthusiasm. More than once a cynical parishioner grumped to me about such a budget, "Why should I come? It's going to be approved anyway." The congregational meeting becomes a rubber stamp on a financial document that just says the church will "keep on keeping on."

Such an approach also encourages a conservative approach to ministry. The safest course a church can chart is one that keeps the same ministries going regardless of whether or not they are achieving their purpose. For example, in one church the Vacation Bible School was a standard line item year after year. Finally, someone asked if VBS ever accomplished its purpose of bringing community persons to Christ. Unfortunately, no one could ever remember a time when it had provided the avenue by which a family had come into fellowship with God and the church. After due consideration Vacation Bible School was shelved for new approaches to evangelism. The change was not easy to make. The way in which the church structured the budget made it easier to hold onto the old than to step forward with the new. Line-item budgets encourage stagnation. It's safer to ask for a 3 percent increase in an existing ministry, regardless of its effectiveness, than to launch a new one that requires a totally new expense.

INTRODUCING THE MISSION BUDGET

How can a church get out of the rut? At Cottonwood reaffirming the link between mission and money provided the key. We discovered that the church budget is not merely a financial product, but a theological document as well. It's important for a church to ask itself whether its professed theology squares with the implicit theology that can be read in the numbers.

Here's what the numbers show in my own congregation. My church is marked by a strong, covenantal theology that affirms our responsibility to the children of the congregation. That's clear from the significant contribution the budget makes to support a Christian day school. My church is also marked by a Presbyterian form of government that stresses the corporate unity of the church. So we earmark a significant amount of the budget for denominational work we do in conjunction with like-minded churches. On the other hand, in spite of my church's expressed commitment to local evangelism, only 2 percent of the budget is directed to the work of the evangelism committee.

Scrutinize your church's budget in the same way. What is the financial theology of your church? To which areas of ministry have you allotted the greatest increases recently? Why? Do those increases square with the long-range goals and objectives of your congregation? Do they reflect your church's stated mission?

A budgeting process that hopes to create any enthusiasm whatsoever on the part of the membership must start with mission and not with money. A healthy budget squares the church's vision with its financial priorities.

DEVELOPING A MISSION BUDGET

If the budget is truly to reflect the mission of the church, the church must know its mission. Without a mission statement and a solid effort to develop goals and objectives that serve the church's mission, a meaningful mission budget will be impossible.

Consequently, a mission budget begins with mission. How does the council intend to move the church forward in its mission next year? What concrete objectives will the church need to make growth a reality? Council does not need to generate dozens of goals and objectives. The 80/20 rule applies here: if 80 percent of the result is determined by 20 percent of the effort, then a few key objectives that can be summarized in several succinct paragraphs will accomplish more than a list that runs on page after page.

Once goals and objectives are set, a tentative budget can be developed. From this perspective the dollars to be spent by the congregation are not so much disbursements as investments. Kennon Callahan points out that "the word 'investment' comes from the Latin verb 'investire,' which means 'to clothe, to put on clothes.' The budget is the clothing we put on the mission" (*Effective Church Finances*, p. 17). Callahan reminds us that there are "human-life costs" as well as "dollar-and-cent" costs which must be taken into account as we budget for the next fiscal year:

> *When you measure costs, measure in lives, not light bulbs. Measure in people, not paper. Measure in mission, not mortar. Measure in help shared, not money conserved. When you think about "costs," think about all the people whose lives will not be richly helped with specific human hurts and hopes. Think about the human costs when we develop an attitude of conserving, holding, preserving, protecting—only increasing the budget a marginal percent per year. What are the costs in your family, in your community, in the country, across the world.*

> —*Callahan,* Effective Church Finances, *p. 20*

If we budget with our eye to our mission, we will avoid the tragedy of saving a dollar but losing a life-changing opportunity to minister in Christ's name.

PUBLICIZING A MISSION BUDGET

Once a mission budget is prepared, the question is how to communicate it to the church. Most finance committees simply share a line-item budget with the congregation. Such a document is a necessary tool for financial management, but it hardly communicates a sense of mission to the congregation. Key goals tend to get lost; consequently, a congregation will find it difficult to see the forest for the trees. A line-item budget often inspires one question: "Why is it costing so much more to do next year what we did this year?"

A council could consider translating the line-item budget into a presentation that will help the congregation understand the people ministry those line items represent. One way to connect money with ministry is to present the budget in terms of the major components of the mission statement, setting up a dollar amount for each aspect of the church's vision statement together with a synopsis of past and future ministry in that area. Appendix B gives an example of what this might look like.

Another approach is to develop a presentation along the lines of the church's goals for the upcoming year. The council could state the goal together with the key objectives that will move the congregation toward reaching that goal. For example, your church may have a major goal to strengthen youth ministry. Objectives that will help achieve that goal may include hiring a part-time staffer, scheduling fall and spring retreats, and developing a small group network. By sharing the goal and objectives in connection with the financial cost, you will link the church's money with the church's ministry.

Always remember—people give to people. When you present the budget as a people budget, you inspire church members to catch the vision.

THE CONGREGATIONAL MEETING

Is your congregational meeting first and foremost a finance meeting? If so, expect those who attend to be those who enjoy picking their way through a line-item budget and asking why the electric bill went up again this year!

Or is your congregational meeting first and foremost a celebration of ministry accomplished and anticipated? I have noted through the years that a missionary reporting on his work in the field draws a noticeably bigger crowd than many congregational meetings devoted to church finance. Why? People are more interested in mission accomplished than in money budgeted.

It's important to use your congregational meeting to tell people how their money got translated into mission: how your church helped people and advanced the cause of Christ through last year's giving. Don't give a *disbursements* report to the congregation; give them an *investment* report, a report about how your giving invested in the lives of people in your church, your community, and the world. Then set out your intended investments for the next year. These are the ways in which you together will advance your church's mission. These are the goals that will help you better to invest your money and yourselves in kingdom treasure that never rusts or corrodes.

Finally, approve a budget that will make such ministry happen. The proposed budget should be the last item on the agenda, not the first. It has its place only after past ministry is celebrated and future ministry is shared. Only then will the budget clearly reflect and affirm our vision of God's plan for us.

In this chapter we have looked at a number of ways we as leaders can share that vision with the congregation as a whole. In the next chapter we will explore ways in which we can share it individually with the members of our church as well.

SESSION SUGGESTIONS
FOR THE LEADER

Scripture Reading: Romans 12:1-13
Reread verses 1-2. Discuss briefly how we will be able to discern what is the will of God—what is "good and acceptable and perfect" (NRSV). How can we find out what God wants us to do as a congregation? How will we know where God wants to lead us? Do verses 3-8 help us to think this through?

Quotable Quotes

Few parishioners are giving anything near their full capability.

A budgeting process that hopes to create any enthusiasm whatsoever on the part of the membership must start with mission and not money. A healthy budget squares the church's vision with its financial priorities.

If the budget is truly to reflect the mission of the church, the church must know its mission. Without a mission statement and a solid effort to develop goals and objectives that serve the church's mission, a meaningful mission budget will be impossible.

A council could consider translating the line-item budget into a presentation that will help the congregation understand the people ministry those line items represent.

Always remember—people give to people. When you present the budget as a people budget, you inspire church members to catch the vision. . . . The proposed budget should not be the first item on the agenda but the last.

Implications and Applications

1. Does your church budget proposal have sufficient drawing power to encourage discussion and active participation on the part of the membership? What improvements could you make?

2. Heerspink sees the church budget as a theological document. What theological statement(s) does your present church budget make? (Leader, be sure to have the budget available in handouts or on overhead so that participants can review it.)

3. How does the 80/20 rule apply to setting financial objectives for your church budget?

4. Is your congregational meeting first and foremost a finance meeting or a celebration of ministry accomplished and anticipated? How can you make it more of the latter?

5. Heerspink suggests two ways in which councils could present the budget to their membership: in terms of major components of the mission statement and along the lines of the church's goals for the upcoming year. Which approach would work best in your church?

Closing Worship

Good leadership requires that we work hard at presenting our ministry vision to our membership in an honest, clear, and inspiring way. But none of that will do much good unless God's Spirit stirs our hearts and the hearts of the people we serve with a genuine desire to follow where our Lord leads us. In your closing worship seek God's guidance and empowerment for your congregation. Pray that "since we live by the Spirit, [we may] keep in step with the Spirit" (Gal. 5:25).

CHAPTER 10

GIVING CAMPAIGNS

I just don't understand the stewardship committee's recommendation to conduct a campaign," John remarks to Dave as they dig into their chocolate cake during the council meeting's coffee break. "It's wrong to ask people how much they intend to give next year. That's a private matter. Besides, don't we trust God anymore to provide the money we need to pay the bills? Doesn't a stewardship campaign show a lack of faith?"

"But look at the other side," Dave answers. "We're $15,000 behind in the general fund. We have to do something! Besides, other organizations do it. The United Way asks for pledges each year. Why shouldn't the church get with the times and go after church dollars the same way?"

This little exchange illustrates the typical battle that looms in council when the question of a Stewardship Week comes up. The lines are drawn between the idealists who believe that the less said about money the better and the realists who are ready to canonize Ben Franklin's dictum: "God helps those who help themselves." Typically, once council makes a decision about a stewardship campaign, one group or the other leaves the table unhappy.

There's a way to cut through the impasse. Despite their differences, John and Dave share a common fallacy: the notion that a stewardship campaign is essentially a fund-raising promotion. Both see the request for pledges as a way of manipulating more money out of members' wallets and into the church's coffers. A stewardship campaign becomes a giant commercial pitched to the congregation. Realists like Dave are ready to accept it as a necessary evil in a day of financial shortfalls. Idealists like John are not.

Both Dave and John need to reassess what a Stewardship Week is all about. It's far more than an attempt to keep the church in the black. Rightly understood, such a campaign is an important invitation to the congregation to grow in discipleship.

REASSESSING OUR APPROACH

In an overall effort launched by Cottonwood Church the stewardship campaign was the most recent element. Why did it lag so far behind other stewardship initiatives? Because Cottonwood, like so many churches, had to overcome its resistance to change. We had to face squarely the weakness of our past practice.

Every congregation has a stewardship campaign of sorts. But many congregations take one of two approaches in the way they conduct it. In the traditional approach council publishes a budget amount. The total church budget is divided by the number of families in the congregation. Council announces this per-family amount to the congregation as the expected level of giving. In such a system adult singles of all ages are left out of the financial calculations—their giving is the slush that allows the church to meet its budget.

This approach suffers from several weaknesses. The one-size-fits-all approach assumes that the congregation is financially homogeneous. But it's not. All congregations have folks who are just scraping by. They also have members who see no reason to prepare a budget because they have so much money that they can't begin to spend it all. Dozens of "giving units" in the average congregation defy classification as families. Asking for contributions according to family tells unmarried singles that their gifts are not important and not expected.

Secondly, the one-size-fits-all approach doesn't square with reality. We often hear that if we all paid forty dollars a week to the budget, we would meet all the church's financial responsibilities. That may be true. But there has been no congregation in history in which everyone gave the same weekly amount. Not a single congregation can produce an end-of-year giving statement that reports the same total for all members. Many members, for one reason or another, are paying much less than the requested budget amount. The implication then is that some members have to give much more than that in order for the church to meet its financial goals. But a per-family budget amount implies that giving more than that is financially heroic. It encourages us to grouse about the fact that we have to pay for those who give less.

Third, the one-size-fits-all approach does not square with Scripture. Our generosity to God's kingdom reflects our spiritual maturity. Some of us have received the gift of giving (Rom. 12:8). Others of us are spiritual infants with a lot of growing up to do in our practice of discipleship. The Bible encourages us to give cheerfully, not grudgingly. We should do so "in proportion to the way the LORD [our] God has blessed [us]" (Deut. 16:17). Such scriptural principles demonstrate the inadequacy of any approach to church funding that expects us all to pay the same dues.

Recognizing the weaknesses of the one-size-fits-all approach, some churches have gone to the opposite extreme. Instead of publicizing an expected level of support, they simply urge, "Give as the Lord has blessed you." These churches offer no guidance whatsoever for congregational giving. That's not helpful either. Most members sincerely want to give intelligently. They want to know the church's need. They want some guidance in establishing a faithful pattern of giving. Therefore, we need to find a third approach.

NEW DIRECTIONS

Some churches invite their members to covenant with God and God's people with respect to their intended giving. This invitation is consistent with the nature of Christian discipleship. When the Bible talks about our identity as Christians, it is very comfortable speaking the language of commitment, promise, and vow. An appropriate stewardship campaign connects our financial lives with the biblical givens. It asks members to plan the disbursement of their money the same way they plan the exercise of other spiritual gifts.

Consider the parishioner who is asked to teach the fifth-grade church school class that meets each Sunday morning. On reflection he or she returns to the superintendent and responds, "I'll do what I can, but I think it is presumptuous of you to expect me to make a commitment to teach for the entire year. After all, my circumstances may change. My company may transfer me out of state. My health might fail. I'll come and teach when I can. But don't expect me to nail down my intentions for the next nine months."

If someone actually talked this way, we would suspect their hesitation had more to do with an unwillingness to face a flock of active fifth graders than with actual fears about possible changed circumstances. Without a significant commitment of time and talent no congregational ministry would remain viable for long. Yet the excuses our potential teacher gives are precisely the arguments many of us give for refusing to make a financial commitment to our church.

God knows better than we do that life is open to sudden and drastic change. The commitment we make to teach in the church school remains conditional upon our God-given physical and emotional resources for carrying out that commitment. But God will not let us escape the call to commitment. A church that doesn't issue that call ignores a very important part of Christian discipleship. And all indications show that Christians respond to such a challenge. People who covenant financially with their church give more: "Studies indicate that members who make estimates of their giving usually give at least 30 percent more than those who do not estimate" (Grimm, *Generous People*, p. 49).

PLEDGES OR ESTIMATES

Grimm goes on to tell the story of a church during the Great Depression that actually sold its members' pledges to the local bank at 90 percent of face value (p. 56). It's that kind of horror story that puts a congregation on its guard when leaders begin to talk about a stewardship campaign. Members wonder just what they are getting into when they are being asked to commit themselves financially during Stewardship Week. They ask what will happen if they fall behind in their giving. Will they end up in debt to the church?

When the stewardship committee of my congregation decided to organize a Stewardship Week, they determined that the word "pledge" was too loaded. In the minds of many members it had legal overtones. Some members feared that if they could not fulfil their pledge, the deacons would present them with a bill.

Instead, the stewardship committee chose to speak of "estimates of giving" (Grimm, p. 48). God ultimately controls our income. If he gives some members more than they expect, then we encourage them to revise their giving upward. If unforeseen financial problems hit, we encourage our members to revise their giving downward. Estimates are moral and spiritual commitments, not legal ones. They form part of our plan for discipleship for the coming year.

Actually, many churches have functioned with a similar approach for years. They ask parishioners for a "faith-promise" commitment for missions. A stewardship campaign simply recognizes that all giving to the church is mission giving and appropriately seeks a faith-promise response on our part.

INGREDIENTS OF A STEWARDSHIP CAMPAIGN

A stewardship campaign does more than just ask church members for dollars. A healthy campaign contains at least five ingredients:

- It teaches the biblical principles.
- It tells the church's story.
- It provides opportunities for members to tell their own stewardship stories.
- It receives the commitments.
- It thanks the congregation.

We'll explore each one of these elements in greater detail.

Teach the Biblical Principles

A basic problem in most churches is that members spell "steward-ship" as "$teward$hip." They hear the word and immediately think of money. A Stewardship Week presents an excellent opportunity to remind the congregation that the word is spelled without those dollar signs. Stewardship is discipleship. It describes our Christian identity. It is an expression of our gratitude to God for giving us Jesus Christ. As Jesus gave his life for us, we, in turn, may gratefully devote our whole lives in service of our Savior and Lord. Our tithing becomes an important means of showing that we are "wholeheartedly willing and ready from now on to live for him" (Heidelberg Catechism, Lord's Day 1).

Tell the Church's Story

The old, old story is always coming to expression in our congregations in new, new ways. Do your members know how that occurs in your church? Count up the number of ministries you have—all of them—from your well-publicized daycare center down to the faithful retiree who, unnoticed, delivers the audiotapes to shut-ins. Don't stop with the "official" activities of the church. Include ministries your parishioners engage in beyond the boundaries of the congregation. Those form part of your congregation's story as well.

Telling the ministry stories of a church does not intend to place its people on a pedestal. It simply affirms the ways in which God is working through the members of Christ's body. *Not* to tell or celebrate your church's mission diminishes the praise that God deserves for his work in and through your congregation.

When you tell the congregation how ministry comes to concrete expression in your church, you encourage good giving. Kenneth Sauer warns, "If you're not up on something, you're likely to be down on it" (Grimm, p. 28). Think of ways to tell the story that go beyond the usual handout or church newsletter. The stewardship committee at Cottonwood assumed that a picture was worth a thousand words in getting its message out. It used the talents of a local television camera operator to prepare a twenty-minute video on Cottonwood's ministries. The committee showed the video to the congregation at the end of a morning worship service. Church members were astonished at what was happening in our church.

Provide Opportunities for Members to Tell Their Own Stewardship Stories

The congregation's story is also made up of the individual stories of its members. Some members of the church will be more seasoned stewards than others. Their stories and accounts of what living a stewardly life can and has meant will serve as an inspiration and guide for younger members who are just beginning to learn good stewardship.

Again, these stories are not intended to put anyone on a pedestal. They are simply beautiful affirmations of the Spirit working in your church family.

Receive the Commitments

Several years ago I asked a long-term member if he was involved in any activities in church. He answered, "None, but then I haven't been asked to do anything either." Involvement in ministry should be a natural response to the gospel. Disciples should respond in obedience regardless of whether they are invited to do so. But many people need to be asked before they participate. Getting people involved in ministry demands more than a nicely worded note in the bulletin. We have to extend a personal request.

A stewardship effort is not complete either until we specifically ask congregation members to covenant with the church about their support of the church's ministries. That can take place in different ways: a letter sent to the members, an estimate-of-giving card, or a personal call. These means all provide ways of asking members to indicate their financial intentions for the coming year. Many good stewardship approaches have floundered because the church failed to ask for a commitment at the critical moment.

Cottonwood Church organized its campaign around a mailing to each church member. It consisted of

- a cover letter explaining our new approach to stewardship (see Appendix C)
- an estimate-of-giving card labeled with the member's name (see Appendix D)
- an envelope in which the estimate-of-giving card could be returned in strict confidentiality to the church

The cover letter explained that the estimate-of-giving cards would be collected during a special offering on the second Sunday of Stewardship Week. The letter encouraged a prompt response by indicating that council members would personally contact those who did not return a card.

It is that element of personal contact that makes many volunteers nervous about participating in a stewardship campaign. The Cottonwood committee shared specific guidelines to help council members keep these contacts on a positive footing (see Appendix E). The committee also took due care in pairing callers with members they were to contact. It's tempting to arrange contacts by geographic location. But that doesn't usually result in the most effective visits.

In our mobile society relational neighborhoods provide a better approach than geographic ones. Such neighborhoods are webs of relationships formed by friendships, common interests, and work. Because they are much more important to people today, it is best to make use of these relational neighborhoods when conducting this kind of campaign. Callers who visit people of similar age, interests, and level of income will be more effective.

In asking for an estimate of giving, it's best to focus on the right question. The issue is not how much the church needs. That's a fund-raising question. The right question is a spiritual one: "How much money does God ask from [you] as a spiritual response of faith?" (Grimm, p. 82). If they keep that in mind, callers will avoid embarrassment when they ask a member for an estimate. They are simply asking a fellow parishioner to take a step of obedient faith.

A church member's response to that invitation brings a sense of joyful freedom. Many people struggle with giving each Sunday. A yearly estimate of giving frees them from that battle. They have thought through their intentions for the coming year. They have committed themselves to financial discipleship.

Thank the Congregation

In most churches the words "Well done, good and faithful servant" are seldom heard. The message that comes through repeatedly is this: "Not bad, but not good enough!" Such an attitude can demoralize both the individual Christian and the church as a whole. If God will one day bless believers with a resounding "Well done," may church leaders be far behind?

Consequently, thank your congregation. Do it publicly as soon as possible after the collection of the estimate-of-giving cards. Don't qualify your thanks by adding that the special collection only reached 67 percent of the goal. More cards may well be on the way. So say, "We are 67 percent of our way toward our financial goal. A big thank-you to all who have given so generously."

DIVERSITY IN A STEWARDSHIP CAMPAIGN

One aim of a stewardship campaign is to put the church on a firm financial footing. But the campaign isn't just concerned with the bottom line. We can highlight various goals from year to year. Stewardship initiatives don't need to look as if they came from the same cookie cutter year after year. Consider these possibilities:

- *Broaden the participation base.* At Cottonwood the goal of our first stewardship campaign was to increase the number of regular givers within the congregation. We wanted the whole congregation to "own" their stewardship role. Our first goal was to encourage *givers* and secondarily to cultivate *giving*. We did not achieve 100 percent participation. But we celebrated a much higher level of participation than the 50 percent most churches experience.

- *Deepen the membership's knowledge of stewardship.* This year your stewardship campaign could involve a special stewardship seminar. How about offering a class in financial planning? Perhaps it's time to expand your Stewardship Week to cover a whole month by offering a series of timely stewardship messages.

- *Grow the congregation's giving.* When your church accepts its stewardship role, challenge it to grow their giving forward. You can issue a specific challenge, such as introducing the concept of a graduated tithe: invite members to offer a tithe in which percentage of giving rises with income (see Appendix F).

- *Issue the grow-one-step challenge.* If a member gives 5 percent of income to the church, challenge him or her to grow a step and give 6 percent. That encourages members to carefully assess their past giving and take an attainable step forward in their stewardship.

- *Present the ninety-day challenge.* Encourage members to commit themselves to a full 10 percent tithe for three months. Focus not only on the call to greater discipleship but also on the opportunity it affords to experience the ways in which God blesses such generous, faithful giving.

YOUR TIMETABLE

Not long ago I browsed through a middle school art festival. Among the submissions was a lovely piece of calligraphy done in colored pencil. The young artist had drawn the alphabet, each letter formed by entwined sunflowers. The work had just one, single flaw. The artist hadn't planned ahead. She began with only four letters on each line. By the time she reached the bottom of the paper she had to cram up to seven letters in each line. My wife, an art teacher, tells me that the biggest challenge of teaching calligraphy is to persuade students to plan ahead.

Such planning is surprisingly hard work. One challenge of a Stewardship Week is developing a workable timetable that incorporates goal setting and budget planning into the campaign.

Most churches plan their Stewardship Week for the fall season to co-incide with a fiscal year that begins January 1. But there is no reason why your fiscal year can't begin on July 1 or on any date that makes sense for your congregation. A fiscal year starting June 1 or September 1 often makes more sense in terms of the flow of the church year. Regardless of when your fiscal year begins, you will need to launch the budgeting process surprisingly early in order to avoid the old pattern of plugging in numbers to maintain the status quo. Appendix G presents a sample time-table for a fiscal year that begins January 1.

A GLORIOUS DEFEAT

So you held your first Stewardship Week. Seventy percent of your congregation pledged 90 percent of the budget. But when you went to the congregation, you announced that there was a commitment from only 140 of your 200 families and that the estimates fell 10 percent short of your goal. Congratulations! You have just snatched defeat from the jaws of victory!

You forgot two things. In an average church only 50 percent of the congregation makes estimates. By enlisting estimates from 70 percent of your congregation, your first Stewardship Week has been a smashing success! Secondly, not all those folks who fail to make an estimate are non-givers. Some may be out of town during Stewardship Week. Others have lingering philosophical objections about making a financial estimate. Yet many of these members will give during the next year—some very generously.

Grimm suggests that we take account of those who do not estimate by doing it for them. Ask those responsible for overseeing the confidential giving records to tally the amount that nonpledgers gave to the church in the previous year. This amount becomes a legitimate addition to your estimates as you finalize your budget.

Once we have our mission budgets in place, and we have challenged our members during Stewardship Week, what will we do for the other fifty-one weeks of the year to encourage congregational giving? That will be our focus in the next chapter.

SESSION SUGGESTIONS
FOR THE LEADER

Scripture Reading: Psalm 50:1-15

Discuss briefly how verses 14 and 15 relate to each other. Then read verse 23. How do these verses still speak to us today?

Quotable Quotes

> Both Dave and John need to reassess what a Stewardship Week is all about. It's far more than an attempt to keep the church in the black. Rightly understood, such a campaign is an important invitation to the congregation to grow in discipleship.

> An appropriate stewardship campaign connects our financial lives with the biblical givens. It asks members to plan the disbursement of their money the same way they plan the exercise of other spiritual gifts.

> Many good stewardship approaches have floundered because the church failed to ask for a commitment at the critical moment.

> In our mobile society relational neighborhoods provide a better approach than geographic ones.

> In asking for an estimate of giving it's best to focus on the right question. The issue is not how much the church needs. That's a fund-raising question. The right question is a spiritual one: "How much money does God ask from [you] as a spiritual response of faith?" (Grimm, p. 82).

Implications and Applications

1. What's wrong with publishing a budget amount, dividing it by the number of families in the congregation, and announcing this per-family amount as the expected level of giving?

2. Do you prefer using "pledge," "estimate of giving," or some other word or phrase to characterize the financial commitment you seek from your members?

3. Heerspink lists four ingredients of a healthy stewardship campaign. What are they? Does your church incorporate them? Should it?

4. How can you keep your yearly stewardship campaigns from looking like they came from a cookie cutter?

5. How can we take account of those who do not estimate by doing it for them?

Closing Worship

Good stewardship arises out of a sincere gratitude to God for providing for us and granting us new life in Christ. Spend some time in thanksgiving and praise. In songs and prayer list the ways in which God has shown you loving-kindness and grace. Petition God to spread these benefits to the needy and those who suffer. Ask God to show love and mercy to them through you and through your church.

CHAPTER 11

GIVING THAT BUILDS MOMENTUM

As Bill calls the stewardship committee to order he observes, "Stewardship Week is over. I guess after we tie up a few odds and ends, our work is done until next year."

"But Bill," asks Sue, "if this is a standing committee, aren't there things we are supposed to be doing throughout the year?"

"Like what? This committee is so new we don't have any precedents. I'm not sure where we can go with this stewardship business until we have to organize our next campaign," Bill replies.

Like Bill many folks wonder what to do about stewardship the other fifty weeks of the year. But if stewardship is a matter of discipleship, we can no more confine it to a single campaign than we can box our mission into a Mission Emphasis Week. Let's explore some ways to keep the stewardship momentum going.

COMMUNICATING WITH THE CONGREGATION

Times have changed. Years ago most congregations were quite satisfied with a unified budget. By combining the funding of dozens of different causes into one general budget, members only needed to write a single check. With that their financial responsibilities to the church were over. Many members had no idea about the causes they were supporting. Many did not care.

Today most parishioners want more accountability from the causes to which they give. They want to give intelligently. As a result we need to communicate seriously on money matters. That communication needs to take place on at least two levels.

First, we need to communicate what the causes are so that church members know about the way their contributions are put to use. A good way to do that is to highlight the work of the general fund by making a "moment for ministry" a monthly event. Such brief reports will show the congregation how important their giving is. Occasionally you may want to invite someone from a denominational mission agency to tell about his or her work as a way of making this moment for ministry very concrete and immediate. Contact the Reformed Church of America's speakers' bureau or Christian Reformed World Missions or World Relief for help in scheduling such visits.

Also consider ways to communicate the nature of the ministries you are supporting through special offerings. Some churches choose in a given year to take more collections for fewer organizations. In this way congregation members begin to learn about the causes they support. You may also want to invite representatives from these organizations to briefly share information about their ministry. Or include a succinct paragraph about the organization in your church bulletin or worship sheet.

A second way we need to communicate is to keep members up to date on their level of giving. Too many churches urge their members for donations but then drop the ball when it comes to keeping them informed about their level of giving throughout the year. We should respect givers sufficiently to keep them well informed. Here are some ways to do that.

1. *Improve the announcements your church places in the bulletin.* Are they timely? Many churches give updates that trail by weeks or even months after the offerings were taken. Consider a biweekly or a weekly report to the congregation. Are your bulletin announcements understandable to the average reader? Financial statements are usually prepared by people with expertise in financial matters. A mini spreadsheet in the bulletin seems clear to them, but it won't fly with the average member who lacks aptitude for financial reports. For years my church reported in the bulletin negative balances by means of dollar amounts set in parentheses. I began asking members if they knew what that meant. Many had absolutely no idea that this was an accountant's notation for shortfall. So we launched a new way of reporting the budget picture—in plain English. If we are a thousand dollars behind, we say that in so many words.

2. *Make up-to-date financial reports available to the congregation.* Many councils manage to get the proposed budget into the hands of every member with timely diligence but make other financial statements almost impossible to get. But if the church's budget is the year's financial game plan, then the six-month statement is the half-time report. And the year-end statement announces the final score! While not everyone in the congregation wants to read through a financial statement, many do. Readily available reports communicate to the congregation that the council operates with financial integrity and keeps no se-

crets. But those reports must be timely: a two-month-old financial statement is as appetizing as yesterday's scrambled eggs.

3. *Distribute regular mailings to the congregation.* Too often church members have no clear idea of how much they have contributed to the church until the end-of-the-year statement arrives. Why not keep them posted on a quarterly basis? Include in the letter a report concerning the financial condition of the church. Share any special financial needs that have arisen. Report members' year-to-date giving along with an expression of appreciation of their financial support. Make sure that the tone of the letter is upbeat and positive.

When it comes to informing the church about stewardship issues, redundancy doesn't hurt. A number of years ago I played in my church's golf league. At the time the budget was about ten thousand dollars in the red. Notices of that unhappy fact appeared at regular intervals in the bulletin, but to little avail. On the links, between slicing one shot and hooking the next, I asked my golf partners to explain why they thought the church was in such a tight financial pinch. They responded, "Shortfall? What shortfall? Why didn't council tell us?"

That situation taught me an important lesson. One little note in the bulletin isn't enough. We need to communicate the church's practice of stewardship in a variety of ways if we want to keep our membership informed.

COORDINATING STEWARDSHIP EFFORTS

A stewardship committee needs to mesh with other committees and organizations in the church in order to encourage stewardship. We have already noted how the stewardship committee needs to interrelate with the finance and executive committees. It can foster other important connections as well. For example, it can

- *serve as a resource to committees raising funds for special projects.* Many churches do not coordinate such efforts, and the bulletin is often crammed with competing pleas for donations. The stewardship committee can serve as a resource to other committees by putting together an effective financial appeal. It can also coordinate fund-raising for special projects. One possibility might be a Christmas wish list in which ministries are invited to post special needs together with dollar costs. The stewardship committee could distribute the wish list to the congregation, allowing members to do some Christmas giving to the causes of their choice.

- *arrange special seminars or classes about stewardship in tandem with the education committee*. To balance stewardship efforts, these classes can be offered at a different time of the year than the stewardship campaign.

- *strategize with the church school and youth ministries about ways to bring the stewardship message to children and youth*. Several excellent resources for children are available. Training the next generation of stewards is one of the greatest challenges facing the church today.

INVOLVING THE CHURCH LEADERSHIP IN STEWARDSHIP

Earlier we stressed that solid stewardship involves leadership by pastor, council, and stewardship committee. In your church encourage the pastor and council to make visioning for greater stewardship part of their ongoing work and to include the message of stewardship in the regular preaching ministry. Urge your pastor to highlight some specific aspect of stewardship six months after the stewardship campaign. Ask the elders to keep stewardship before the congregation in their contacts with church members. Challenge the deacons to work hard at promoting stewardship. There are excellent tools available to help them do so. CRC Publications and the RCA Distribution Center will be glad to suggest resources.

KEEP THE FRESH IDEAS COMING

Your church newsletter can become an important vehicle for keeping stewardship before your congregation. What about having a regular column for stewardship ideas? The following are some concrete suggestions about what you could include.

- *Encourage members to establish a separate investment account for their charitable giving*. One family I know has an account called "God's Checkbook." Family members immediately deposit the portion of their income they earmark for donations. Then they distribute funds as the needs of various ministries come to their attention.

- *Encourage members to increase their giving in proportion to the increase in their life expenditures*. For example, if the number of their vacations has gone from one to two a year, perhaps it's time for them to consider a similar increase in giving.

- *Encourage members to consider a "kingdom portfolio" of stewardship investment*. Because kingdom needs come in such a wide variety of categories—denominational, evangelistic, diaconal, international—they warrant a diversified portfolio. Giving to a broad range of causes develops a holistic understanding of God's work in the world.

- *Encourage members to broaden their stewardship beyond their giving*. Ask members to list the causes to which they regularly give; then encourage them to pray regularly for those ministries. Ask them to volunteer their time and talent as well.

In this chapter we have had a chance to reflect on ways in which we can promote stewardship all year long, not just one week of the year. Beyond that, as we shall see, we can also provide our members with the opportunity to keep on giving even after they themselves are long gone.

PAYING ATTENTION TO PLANNED GIVING

The stewardship committee meeting had ended. As the committee members gathered up the coffee cups, Frank mentioned an article he had recently scanned in the newspaper. "Trillions of dollars in assets are going to change hands over the next few decades. No generation has ever had so much wealth to leave to its children."

"Funny how none of that money ever seems to find its way into our church treasury," replied Doug. "We have five or six funerals a year here at Zion Church. But I can't remember the church receiving a single bequest."

Frank agreed, "Just shows you how people take their church for granted."

Frank may be right. Or maybe the church should shoulder some of the blame because it has ignored the possibility of planned giving. What would happen if a sizeable bequest materialized next week at your church? Would your council have any idea what to do with it? Or would this windfall simply lead to rounds of bickering as various church factions try to seize control of those dollars for their own projects?

WHY YOUR CHURCH NEEDS AN ENDOWMENT FUND

Through the years I've heard disparaging comments about congregational endowment funds. Occasionally a horror story surfaces of a church with an endowment fund so massive that church leadership no longer needs to pay attention to the congregation. So much money flows from the endowment that it is immaterial whether people give or not.

I can imagine that an ill-conceived, poorly executed endowment fund can be a detriment to a congregation. Yet in such situations the problem isn't with the endowment fund itself but with the quality of leadership within the congregation. An endowment fund doesn't need to be a drag on congregational stewardship. It can become the foundation of the overall stewardship program. An endowment fund can provide the funds to carry a church to levels of ministry that would otherwise far exceed its reach.

An endowment fund may seem to make little sense when your people aren't including the church in their wills. Maybe no one has ever left your church a bequest or taken out a life insurance policy with the church as the beneficiary. You may ask, "Then why do we need an endowment fund?"

The answer is that it is precisely because those gifts are *not* flowing in your direction! Most churches haven't established a vehicle for planned giving. They haven't done the groundwork that will encourage their parishioners to remember their church through planned gifts. Without an established endowment fund, prospective donors may be reluctant to leave a significant bequest to their church. They will have legitimate concerns about how it will be used.

Consider Pete and Marge, a typical couple who are planning their will. They decide to include "a child named Charity." They have two daughters and a son but intend to split their estate four ways. This leaves one fourth for causes in God's kingdom. What causes should they designate in their will? Folks like Pete and Marge typically channel their planned gifts to organizations they have supported over the years. They have given generously to Bethel Church for thirty-five years. They were married at Bethel and have been members ever since. They consider bequeathing a large sum of money to Bethel, but they are perplexed about what the church will do with it. Pete and Marge really don't want to dictate a special project to the church. How can they possibly determine a sensible use for their gift years in advance?

On the other hand, just leaving their money to the general fund seems equally unappealing. After all, this gift is the fruit of a lifetime of labor and saving. A major gift to the general fund seems to them like granting a year's tax relief to the rest of the congregation. After due consideration Marge and Pete decide to channel their bequest to three denominational causes: diaconal ministry, mission outreach, and higher education.

Consider another scenario. Henry and Judy are members of Hope Church. Their church has an endowment fund with a clear policy on how it will distribute such proceeds. It uses these dollars to embark on projects that would otherwise lie well beyond the church's financial means. A third of the money underwrites scholarships for families who need help sending their children to the Christian school. The fund earmarks another third for community ministry. And it designates a third for world mission support.

Since they have supported their church faithfully for the past twenty years, Henry and Judy decide that it makes sense to keep giving after they are gone. They know that their gift is going to make a difference at Hope Church indefinitely. In their will Henry and Judy include a generous gift to Hope's endowment fund.

FACING THE KEY QUESTIONS

As you contemplate an endowment fund for your congregation, there are several sets of questions that need careful answers. First there are structural questions: Who will administer the fund? Should there be a separate entity, or can an existing committee take on this task? While an existing committee might be able to oversee the fund, there is merit in establishing a separate organizational structure to give the endowment fund some independence. An able as well as stable governing committee will inspire confidence that encourages this important means of giving. However, the church council should make all decisions concerning the distribution of endowment fund income.

Other questions that may arise relate to the kinds of gifts that will be solicited and channeled into the endowment fund: Will you seek only bequests? Will the church take steps to encourage members to give to the endowment fund in life as well as in death? There are a variety of ways they can give while they are still living.

Finally, you will need to clarify how the funds will be distributed. Endowment income should never underwrite basic operating expenses. That situation would discourage giving to the fund and could well undercut the regular giving of the congregation. Instead, the church should develop a clear spending policy. In *Effective Church Finances* Kennon Callahan suggests three criteria for evaluating the projects an endowment fund underwrites: balance, integrity, and broad-based appeal.

First, your church should make sure it balances disbursements among a number of possible causes. Don't channel all endowments to bricks and mortar. Don't pour them all into new church development. Strike a sensible balance. Secondly, select projects that have the integrity to elicit the trust of your congregation. Finally, consider projects that have broad-based appeal. Keeping in mind your congregational history, identify projects that will have grassroots support among your members (Callahan, p. 141-42).

INITIAL AND ONGOING SUPPORT

In one of my churches council established a perpetual organ fund. As far as I know, it had a balance of exactly zero dollars. In fact, I don't believe that it has ever received a single dollar in gifts. Apart from the fact that it may not be a good idea to establish a perpetual fund for a specific item that may someday no longer be needed, I suspect that council itself has long ago forgotten the fund even exists. That's because the organ fund has never been faithfully publicized or promoted. Once established, it disappeared—along with so many good intentions—into that black hole we call the council minutes.

Your endowment fund will likely do the same thing if you not make plans to promote it faithfully. This task alone offers a strong reason to entrust its oversight to a separate committee whose members have both financial and people sense. Some ideas for keeping your endowment before the congregation include the following:

- *Encouraging annual membership gifts to the endowment fund.* Establish a modest level for membership in the fund of perhaps $25 per individual or $50 per family. If you do that, you leave the door open for broad participation. By allowing your members to identify with the endowment fund through regular giving, you encourage them to take the next stewardship step by making a planned gift to the fund.

- *Extend your reach.* Your endowment fund need not be funded only by members of your congregation. If your church is doing ministry that impacts the community, there may well be others, such as former members or friends, who would like to make a lasting gift to your congregation. You can also encourage people to designate memorial and commemorative gifts to the endowment fund.

- *Schedule one offering a year for the endowment fund.* Consider doing so on a special occasion such as Thanksgiving.

- *Publicize your endowment fund by developing an appropriate brochure.* Include it in the information packet that new members receive and mail it to all members at least every other year. If you offer new members' classes, make sure that you include an explanation of the endowment fund as well.

- *Publicize the ministry that happens through grants made by your endowment fund.* Make sure that your congregation appreciates the difference your endowment fund is making in the church and community.

- *Schedule regular programs that encourage your members to make a will and that help them to consider avenues for planned giving.*

- *Keep the endowment fund before the congregation.* You could plan an annual dinner promoting the fund and enjoy good fellowship while you report on the benefits of endowment income to your church and community. Be sure to thank those who have given in the past. Explain the endowment's ground rules and ask for continued, generous support of the fund in the year ahead.

KINDS OF GIFTS

When we speak of endowment funds, we usually think of two kinds of gifts: cash gifts and bequests. But there are many other avenues of giving to be encouraged. The following are among the possibilities:

- *Stocks and bonds*. Such appreciated assets can be transferred to the endowment fund. Doing so often provides significant tax advantages to the donor.

- *Retirement plan assets*. In some cases testamentary gifts of this type of asset avoid estate and income taxes of up to 75-80 percent.

- *Real estate*. A gift of real estate may avoid potentially significant capital gains taxes on appreciated property.

- *Gift annuities*. A gift annuity is a legal contract between the giver and the local church. In return for a gift of cash, appreciated assets, or other property, the recipient receives a fixed annual income for life. This income is based on age and the amount of the gift. A gift annuity can be deferred, with payments to begin at a designated date in the future. Payments may also be designated to a survivor for the rest of his/her life.

- *Life insurance*. Donors can assign or purchase a life insurance policy, naming the endowment fund as the beneficiary. Tax benefits for these kinds of gifts make them a very attractive option.

ORGANIZATIONS TO ASSIST YOUR PLANNING EFFORTS

If you want more information about planned giving, consider the services of the Barnabas Foundation (United States), Christian Stewardship Services (Canada), and the RCA Foundation. These organizations can help your church encourage planned giving by offering advice and by making presentations on stewardship opportunities, such as will and estate planning. These organizations also work directly with individuals in the areas of will-making, tax and estate planning, and income-generating gifts. They offer these services on a no-fee and no-obligation basis. In the United States the RCA Foundation represents agencies related to the Reformed Church in America and the Barnabas Foundation represents agencies related to the Christian Reformed Church. In Canada Christian Stewardship Services represents the agencies related to both of these churches.

Here's how to reach these services:

Barnabas Foundation
15127 S. 73rd Ave., Suite G
Orland Park, IL 60462
(708)532-3444; Fax: (708)532-1217
Executive Director: David Vander Ploeg

Christian Stewardship Services
455 Spadina Ave., 210
Toronto, ON M5S 2G8
(416)598-2128; Fax: (416)977-4611
Executive Director: Harry Houtman

RCA Foundation
1790 Grand Boulevard
Schenectady, NY 12309
(800)766-9660
Coordinator of Gift Planning: Norman Tellier

STEWARDLY LIVES

In this chapter we have covered a lot of ground. We have explored avenues of giving that extend not only over a week or even a year, but also over an entire lifetime and beyond. Our good God showers us with blessings from cradle to grave, gives us Jesus Christ, empowers us with the Holy Spirit, and promises us an inheritance the world cannot even begin to dream about. Our riches in giving should gratefully reflect the riches of our Lord, given to every one of us. To God be the glory.

SESSION SUGGESTIONS FOR THE LEADER

Scripture Reading: Matthew 25:31-46

Who are "the least of these brothers of mine" (v. 40)? What determines the differing destinations described in verse 46? Is Jesus teaching works-righteousness here?

Quotable Quotes

> Today most parishioners want more accountability from the causes to which they give. They want to give intelligently. As a result we need to communicate seriously on money matters.

> Too many churches urge their members for donations but then drop the ball when it comes to keeping them informed about their level of giving throughout the year.

> When it comes to informing the church about stewardship issues, redundancy doesn't hurt.

> An endowment fund doesn't need to be a drag on congregational stewardship. It can become the foundation of the overall stewardship program. An endowment fund can provide the funds to carry a church to levels of ministry that would otherwise far exceed its reach.

> Endowment income should never underwrite basic operating expenses. That situation would discourage giving to the fund and could well undercut the regular giving of the congregation.

Implications and Applications

1. How could your church do a better job of keeping members well-informed and up to date about their giving?

2. How does your church's stewardship committee (or other agency responsible for stewardship) network with other committees? How can you be sure that actually happens?

3. How can council ensure that stewardship visioning remains an on-going agenda item?

4. What do you think of the idea of scheduling elder-deacon teams to conduct family visits? Would that be useful in your church? If you have had experience with such visits, what was the result?

5. Does your council have a policy concerning what to do with bequests? How do you encourage such giving?

6. Should your church endowment fund be administered by a separate board? If so, how should it relate to council?

Quo Vadis?

As church leaders you have had a concentrated look at the importance of stewardship in the life of the church and of every believer. In order to make this study productive, it's important that you follow up on that information. You may wish to do more study. You may wish to make some changes in your church, from a minor tune-up to an entire overhaul. As you discuss where you go from here, be sure to review the concrete suggestions that your clerk or reporter has recorded during your sessions: How will these suggestions appear on your agenda in a way that you can productively deal with them? Councils who have dared to tackle the issue of stewardship from a biblical perspective have seen their churches benefit greatly. May this be true for you as well.

Closing Worship

In closing worship give thanks for what you have discovered about biblically faithful stewardship and giving. Confess where you fall short and ask for God's healing and forgiveness. Ask God to lead you on as you continue to provide leadership in this important area of service in your church. Above all, pray for the riches of God's grace and Spirit for your congregation so that your church may share with those whom your Lord calls you to serve.

EPILOGUE

The first snowflakes were just beginning to fly in my home state of Michigan when I flew to Florida to attend a conference of the Ecumenical Center for Stewardship Studies. This conference promised to be something special. Usually when church leaders talk about the stewardship practice of the church, the information is anecdotal. This conference brought together people with data to back up their conclusions. For three days social researchers reported on extensive scientific studies that separate myth from reality on the topic of church giving.

Researcher Dean Hoge challenged us to assess the deepest reasons for our giving. He noted that some people give as a tradeoff with God: they give to God to make sure that God keeps giving to them. In its crassest form this motive degenerates into a health-and-wealth gospel.

Others give primarily because of the rewards they will reap in their community. Secular fund-raisers often effectively tap this motive. A large gift raises their standing in the eyes of others. They give, but the reputation they purchase for themselves is worth their investment.

Then there are those who give only because the causes are extensions of themselves. They fund their child's service project. They give to their college alma mater. They give only because their self-identity is caught up in their child's future or their school's reputation.

Hoge argues that, for the Christian, giving must have a deeper motive: thankfulness. Grateful giving is probably the form of giving we practice least. Yet it is the most appropriate one for believers who are thankful for the manifold gift-giving of their God.

This is the kind of giving that marks *Firstfruits Congregations*. It is giving that bubbles forth like an artesian well. It cannot be contained. It's motivated by the sheer joy of the good news of Jesus Christ. May you find yourself part of such a Firstfruit Congregation, where giving comes as naturally to your discipleship as does your receiving of our Lord's grace.

SUGGESTIONS FOR STEWARDSHIP MESSAGES

FAITHFUL STEWARDS: MATTHEW 25:14-30

People today are confused about the meaning of the word "steward-ship." In a recent study 40 percent of Americans considered stewardship to be using talents in a responsible way. Sixteen percent thought it meant remembering that God made everything. Twelve percent believed it was taking good care of the planet. Ten percent understood it to mean giving a certain percentage of their money to the church. And 20 percent simply admitted they didn't know what the word meant (Wuthnow, p. 143).

The struggle to define stewardship grows from a realization that it involves all of the above—and more. In Jesus' parable of the talents we find three essential elements of stewardship.

Entrusted Responsibility

This parable is one of several in which Jesus describes discipleship as a form of stewardly servanthood (see Luke 16:1-9; Luke 17:7-10; Matt. 18:23-35; Matt. 20:1-16; Matt. 21:28-32). A key aspect of the parable is the high degree of responsibility entrusted to the servant because the landlord has gone away. It illustrates that we need to counterbalance our affirmation that God is "with us always, even to the end of the age": we need to frankly admit that God is not visibly present in ordinary life. Our servanthood takes place in an age in which the risen Christ has physically gone "into a far country." As we await his return upon the clouds of heaven, faithfulness becomes our responsibility as his stewards.

Entrusted Resources

The need for faithfulness resides in the nature of the resources entrusted to the servant. They remain the Master's possession. The servant, in charge of much, owns nothing. And the size of the trust varies from servant to servant. We are not "created equal" when it comes to the resources God places under our care.

This parable underscores the immense wealth God has entrusted to every steward. A talent was ten thousand denarii. Since a denarius was the daily wage of the ordinary worker, ten thousand denarii constitutes a sum equal to approximately thirty-five years of day labor! These fortunes are specifically entrusted to the steward for his use until the master returns. The Greek text emphasizes the speed with which the first two servants respond. "Immediately" stands at the beginning of the Greek sentence structure in verse 16. The first two servants make it their first priority to use their master's resources.

A Final Accounting

The concept of stewardship can be meaningful only if there comes a day of reckoning. That day comes at the master's return. The basis for the judgment of the third steward is faithfulness.

We tend to judge this man harshly until we put ourselves in his place. After all, he had been entrusted with the least. When issued a challenge, don't our less gifted friends often protest that more able people should respond first? Moreover, this steward certainly cannot be accused of squandering his talent. He has kept it carefully hidden in a cloth. No one can accuse him of wasting his master's wealth. He's not like the prodigal whose riotous living soon exhausted his father's inheritance.

To cap it off, this steward even has a theological reason for his reluctance. His master reaps where he does not sow. So the master certainly does not need the steward's feeble efforts in order to add to his vast estates. In the face of such a powerful man, how could the steward possibly dare to run the risk of losing that talent by using it!

So it shocks us when this outwardly humble man gets condemned as wicked and lazy and pronounced fit only to be hurled into hell. But consider this: by his disobedience the lazy steward shows his master how little he thinks of his master's grace. Frederick Bruner says it well: "Jesus thinks of our work as a million-dollar opportunity to show our high or low view of him" (*Matthew, a Commentary*, p. 903). Such million-dollar opportunities still come to each of us every day.

Suggested Songs of Response

The song suggestions for these sermons can be found in *The Psalter Hymnal* of the Christian Reformed Church; *Rejoice in the Lord*, the hymnal of the Reformed Church of America; and *Songs for LiFE*, a hymnal for children published by CRC Publications to accompany its LiFE church school curriculum.

"We Give You But Your Own" — PsH 296; RL 427
"Thank You, God, for Soil, Water and Air" —PsH 437
"The Wise May Bring Their Learning" —SFL 70

Action Idea

To reinforce this message, you may want to include the following invitation in the liturgy:

Stewardship has many facets. It extends far beyond our financial wealth. Take some time to reflect upon your identity as a steward, then list the concrete ways God has appointed you to be a steward in the following areas:

- my stewardship of material resources
- my stewardship in personal relationships
- my vocational stewardship
- my stewardship of the gospel of Jesus Christ

CHRIST AND CREDIT: PROVERBS 22:7

"I owe, I owe, so off to work I go" is a bumper sticker with a great deal of truth. Americans owe a great deal. Ron Blue, a Christian financial advisor, points out that "the payment of installment debt in 1950 represented 10 percent of the average family's disposable income. In the 1980s that figure had risen to 20-23 percent" (*The Debt Squeeze*, p. 5). Most people carrying such a debt load don't just fail to save for their future, they find it impossible to give to their church as well.

The Modern Cast to the Issue

Of course debt is as old as civilization itself. But debt as we experience it today is very much a modern phenomenon. No society has ever had the easy credit that ours enjoys. No economic system has ever allowed people to live so far beyond their means. As one writer notes, "Some people possess a lot but don't own very much." This seemingly impossible situation has become a reality in our credit-oriented world. The mass media assure us that the use of credit is good, an option any successful person should seize.

A Biblical Perspective on Debt

Proverbs provides the raw material needed to develop a healthy perspective on the use of credit. The very existence of wisdom literature reminds us that our lives must be informed not only by faith and love but also by wisdom. We must respect Old Testament wisdom literature for what it is. Proverbs are not guarantees on life. They are wise sayings reflecting truths that conform to the nature of God's world.

We must be careful not to use this proverb to argue that Christians may *never* borrow money. Scripture does not support the argument that it is sinful to borrow in *any* situation. We must balance Romans 13: 8, often quoted to condemn all borrowing, against other texts (Ex. 22:25; Ps. 37:26; Matt. 5:42).

But this proverb offers wise advice when we face a situation in which we must consider the use of credit. Simply put, debt is dangerous. The proverb gives the reason: a loan changes the relationship between borrower and lender. Money has leverage. There is something about debt that enslaves us (see Neh. 5:4, 5). Because borrowing money makes us servants to the institution from which we borrowed, our lives are not quite our own. Our decisions must be made in the light of our debts. Consequently, many of us forego giving to God's kingdom because we owe the bank. Or we find our opportunities to volunteer our time severely restricted because our debt forces us to take second jobs. Debt places us at the disposal of the lender.

Some Practical Guidelines

How can we determine if our debt is legitimate? Ron Blue offers some helpful guidance, pointing out that there are four typical reasons why Americans often end up in debt:

- lack of discipline
- lack of contentment
- search for security
- search for significance

All four violate basic principles of how a disciple of Christ should live. Failing to exercise discipline over our finances is just plain sloppy stewardship. Seeking to find contentment, security, or significance in what easy credit provides denies that all three of these realities can ultimately be found only in our relationship with Jesus Christ.

Conclusion

Among the sayings of the Desert Fathers is the story of an important dignitary who gave a basket of gold pieces to a priest in the desert, asking him to disperse it among the brethren. "They have no need of it," replied the priest. The wealthy benefactor insisted and set the basket of coins at the doorway of the church, asking the priest to tell the brethren,

"Who so hath need, let him take it." No one touched it or even cared enough to look. Edified and no doubt astonished, the dignitary left with his basket of gold.

—Freedom of Simplicity, *Foster, p. 57*

Compare that episode to the sign in a public library: "Please! Do not leave your belongings unattended!" G. K. Chesterton once said, "There are two ways to get enough; one is to continue to accumulate more and more. The other is to desire less" (Foster, p. 110). Good advice for a credit-crazed world like ours!

Suggested Songs of Response
"The Lord's My Shepherd, I'll Not Want" —RL 89, 90
"My Shepherd Will Supply My Need" —PsH 550
"He Leadeth Me" —PsH 452; RL 161

Action Idea
Consider including the following in your worship sheet:

Are You in Control of Your Debt Load?
True or False:
- Above and beyond a mortgage, you need credit to live.
- You rarely pay off your entire monthly credit-card bill.
- A quarter or more of your income goes to paying off credit-card bills.
- You use one credit card to pay off another.
- You have more than three credit cards.
- You do not have enough income to pay your bills.
- You fail to keep track of your purchases.
- You need your credit card to pay for essentials.
- Having access to credit makes you feel richer.
- You fail to inform your spouse of your spending.
- You don't know how much interest you're paying on overdue credit accounts.

More than four trues and you need to seriously question how stewardly you are in handling credit. If you answered more than half of them true, run, don't walk, to someone who can help you to structure your finances in a more biblically obedient way.

MACEDONIAN GIVING: 2 CORINTHIANS 8:1-15

This passage contains Paul's instructions to the Corinthian church regarding *The Great Collection*. With this collection for the poor of Jerusalem he intends to demonstrate the solidarity of the Christian church. Paul sees it as a concrete expression of the mystery of God, now revealed in the body of Christ. The dividing wall of hostility between Jew and Gentile has been reconciled through the cross of Christ (Eph. 2:14-16).

When we understand that theological realities are present whenever a collection is taken, then we begin to see why the collection has an appropriate place in our worship service. The offering plate is not an intrusion into worship but an integral part of Christian discipleship. To teach the Corinthians that truth, Paul introduces them to a remarkable congregation. He encourages them, and us, to give like a Macedonian.

The Macedonian Model of Giving

While the Corinthians had made a good beginning in this collection (2 Cor. 8:10), their efforts have stalled. Fearing embarrassment upon his arrival, Paul spurs the church to further action by offering a model of exemplary giving: the church in Macedonia. Paul underlines several qualities of its giving.

First, despite personal poverty the Macedonian believers give in a shockingly generous manner. They literally give "beyond their ability" (2 Cor. 8:3). Generous giving is possible for every believer because generosity is defined not by what we give but by what we keep for ourselves (see 8:12).

Secondly, the Macedonians' giving is spontaneous and joyful. They demonstrate the "hilarity" that God seeks in people (2 Cor. 9:7). Paul tells us that the Macedonians beg him for the privilege of participating in this collection for Jerusalem (8:4). When relating the Macedonian model, he specifically reminds the Corinthians that he refuses to give a legalistic command regarding their giving. Instead, he expects them to spontaneously embrace the principle of equality: "your plenty will supply what they need, so that in turn their plenty will supply what you need" (8:14). Paul considers such giving to be the pattern for all his churches.

The Prerequisite to Macedonian Giving

An explanation for this remarkable behavior is necessary, and Paul supplies it in 2 Corinthians 8:5: "They gave themselves first to the Lord and then to us." Here is the key to Macedonian giving. The giving of self precedes the giving of wealth. We put ourselves in the collection plate before we drop in our money. There is no true giving to God without our personal embrace of the great Reformed confession: "I am not my own, but belong body and soul to my faithful Savior, Jesus Christ" (Heidelberg Catechism, Q&A 1).

This self-giving involves giving ourselves to God. In the process it also includes giving ourselves to the ministry of the church. We frequently forget the words "and then to us" (v. 5) in our exposition of this passage. A commitment to Christ implicitly demands a commitment to the body of Christ and to the work that Christ through that body continues to accomplish in the world.

Several Macedonians appear in the New Testament as sterling examples of self-giving. There's Aristarchus, who accompanied Paul on his last journey to Rome. The only way he could accompany Paul the prisoner was to enroll as a slave himself. He literally "gave himself." Then there was Epaphroditus. Bringing Paul a gift from Philippi, he came near death for the sake of Christ's work. He also "gave himself." Only as we still "give ourselves" today will we be able to give generously and freely to the ministries of God's kingdom.

The Grace Sustaining Macedonian Giving

But isn't such self-giving impossible? Yes it is—apart from the God who has given so much. Paul specifically connects the possibility of Macedonian giving with God's grace. Paul begins by noting that he wants us to know about the "grace that God has given the Macedonian churches" (8:1). Later he expresses the hope that the Corinthians will excel in the "grace of giving" (8:7). Paul connects this grace with the example of Christ, who, being rich, became poor for our sakes (8:9).

So giving is not merely something we do for God. It's something that God does through us. It takes the freeing grace of God to work the self-giving that makes us able to turn our Sunday "tip" into generous gifts.

Suggested Songs of Response

"For the Fruits of His Creation" —RL 21; PsH 455
"Christian Hearts in Love United" —PsH 513
"Sing Alleluia" —SFL 68

Action Idea

Often church members know little about where their contributions go. How much do you know about the monies received for the ministries of your denomination? Do some research: make a list of the causes and the amounts spent on each. Find out why each of them is important and be sure, during the coming week, to pray for each of these ministries individually, and especially the people involved in them.

A SAMPLE STEWARDSHIP BUDGET

Here is a sample of the way in which Cottonwood Heights Church presented its 1996 budget.

TITLE PAGE

Vision '96
Cottonwood Heights Church
Annual Report

PAGE 1

From the Pastor

Dear Congregation,

Sometimes when we talk about money, we say one thing and mean another. For example, I come home from the sidewalk sale with my arms filled with packages and a smile on my face. "Honey," I shout up the stairs, "come down and see all the money I saved." My spouse, of course, is more likely to think of the money I spent than the money I saved. It's doubtful that we can really save money by spending it. We say one thing. We mean another.

Perhaps it's that way when it comes to church budgets. We look at the proposed budget for 1996 and think of it in terms of planned disbursements—money to be spent. Yet at a deeper level the dollars that are represented in this report are not disbursements but investments. The word "investment" comes from the Latin verb *investire*, which means "to clothe—to put clothes on." In a real way the budget is the clothing we put on the mission we intend to carry out for the sake of Christ's kingdom. In our financial planning we should take human-life costs into account as well as dollar-and-cent costs. When we measure in human-life costs, we realize that a lack of mission investment has its own cost: mission that is left unaccomplished!

As I look at our budget, I do not merely see expenditures. I see investment in God's mission. I see visits made to hurting people. I see covenant children nurtured in the faith. I see the Jenison community visited with the gospel of Christ. I see Christians in training for more effective discipleship. I see remarkable investments in God's kingdom.

God calls us to faithful financial stewardship. May God bless our kingdom investments in the year ahead.

In Christ's service,
Pastor Bob

PAGE 2

From the Stewardship Committee

The 1996 budget continues Cottonwood's new approach to stewardship begun last fall as we held our first Stewardship Week. This report intends to answer some basic questions about this process.

Why did council feel such an approach was needed? In the past the yearly proposed budget was developed with no input from the congregation as far as funding that budget was concerned. For several years our general fund ran a deficit. Your council believed that a more meaningful budget process would tie our financial stewardship into the budget process itself.

What is the new approach that council has developed? Our council begins the budget process by developing a potential budget for the next fiscal year. Council then asks members to estimate their level of financial support for the upcoming year. On the basis of these estimates the stewardship committee recommends to council an expected income upon which to base the budget. Council then proposes a budget based on this recommendation to the congregation.

How effective has this new approach been? With the end of the fiscal year still a month away, our giving has not only met but exceeded the estimate upon which we based the 1995 budget. Dollars collected in excess of the 1995 budget will be used to meet the shortfall on our obligations.

Council gives thanks for the significant step forward in financial stewardship, represented by the budget before you.

OUR SUPPORT STAFF AND EXPENSES

In order for a congregation to follow the call of its great shepherd, Jesus Christ, it must be led by an under-shepherd. In addition to the work of our senior pastor, there is the need for support ministry to sustain his work and the work of our various committees. Our church office is a busy place, as all of you who drop in during the week already know.

[*list of salaries and office expenses*]

Our investment in this portion of our ministry is [*amount*].

COTTONWOOD HEIGHTS—CELEBRATING GOD'S GRACE

Worship is at the heart of our life together. In worship we celebrate the grace Jesus has shown us. Our worship is a blend of song, prayer, and the spoken Word, which brings glory to God and edifies God's people.

From our Pastor:

> *Cottonwood Heights Church exists to praise and worship God. This past year a bell choir added a new dimension of praise to our worship. Senior and junior choirs, our praise-and-worship teams, and a variety of musical groups all contribute to the celebration here at Cottonwood. We seek to incorporate the various aspects of the service into a meaningful whole. Central to our worship is a focus on the Word of God. I seek to carefully study and present the meaning of the sermon text and to apply it to our lives in a culturally relevant way.*

> *Pastor Bob*

The following expenses are necessary for our worship experience:

[*list of worship expenses*]

Our investment in this ministry is [*amount*].

COTTONWOOD HEIGHTS—CULTIVATING FAITH

Together we as a church are committed to growing spiritually. This involves an active ministry program for our children and young people as well as educational opportunities for our adult members. Our ministries include [list of ministries].

From our Youth Directors:

> *As a youth group our goal is to have an outreach program through group activities, a time for spiritual growth through our Living Groups and Bible study, and a time to serve through our mission projects. This past year we collected food for Roosevelt Park food pantry, served the homeless at Casey's Restaurant, and went to Missouri to help with flood relief. Again this year we will be collecting food, serving the homeless, and going on a service project this coming spring break. A spring paint spree is also planned. Our ultimate goal for the youth group is to expose teens*

in a positive way to Christ and to help students build a relationship with Jesus, which will result in their going out to serve him.

Your Directors

The following costs are involved with our educational and youth ministry programs:

[*list of salaries and expenses*]

Our investment in this portion of our ministry is [*amount*].

COTTONWOOD HEIGHTS—CARING IN LOVE

[*The pastoral care ministry and the other ministries of the congregation are presented in the same way, as are proposed commitments to regional and denominational ministries and debt reduction.*]

WHY GIVE?

Like any organization, a church has expenses that must be met. But we give not just to pay the bills. Here are some other reasons:

1. We give to bring glory and honor to God as we respond to God's call to financial stewardship: "You glorify God by your obedience to the confession of the gospel of Christ and by the generosity of your sharing " (2 Cor. 9:13).

2. Systematic and consistent giving acknowledges God's ownership and makes clear our role as stewards: "What did you have that you did not receive? And if you did receive it, why do you boast as though you did not?" (1 Cor. 4:7).

3. Our giving enables individuals and organizations to meet the needs of God's people.

4. Giving benefits *us*. Christ said there is more blessing in giving than in receiving (Acts 20:35).

5. Giving is an excellent, credible testimony of our faith to churched and unchurched people alike.

LETTER EXPLAINING THE NEW APPROACH TO STEWARDSHIP

[*Date*]

Dear Congregation Member:

God intends us to advance the kingdom with the financial resources placed at our disposal. This past year our stewardship efforts have sought to highlight that link between money and ministry. We are grateful that many congregation members are developing a better understanding of giving. The knowledge that stewardship constitutes an important part of our spiritual worship is spreading.

The next two Sundays will provide us with an opportunity to reflect on our giving for the upcoming year. During our Stewardship Week you will be given an opportunity to make an estimate of your giving for next year. We provide this opportunity because we are convinced that God has financially blessed us to different degrees. It follows that the Lord calls us to prayerfully decide how large our financial commitment to the church should be. Because we want to plan for next year in an orderly way, we are informing our membership now of our stewardship intentions.

A few weeks ago council met to draft a general fund budget which supports these specific areas of ministry:

- the local ministries of our congregation
- denominational and regional ministries
- [*other ministries*]

Our goal for the general fund for next year is [*amount*]. In addition to our general fund our building-fund budget for next year is [*amount*]. Our stewardship goal (general and building funds) is [*amount*].

There are two things you should know about this total goal. First, it includes [*percentage amount*] payment of classis (regional synod) and denominational commitments. The total amount of our commitment to denominational ministry for next year is [*amount*].

A second thing you should know is that this budget envisions growth in support of local youth programs. Council would like to expand funding in these areas so that youth leaders can focus more on doing this important ministry and less on fund-raising for it. The tentative budget drafted by council will expand our expenditures in this area by approximately [amount].

Council asks that in the next few days you take the following steps:

- First, prayerfully consider what your firstfruit giving should be for the upcoming year. We ask that every member consider a commitment of at least 6 percent of gross income to the ministries of our church. We praise the Lord that many members are giving beyond that level. While stewardship is a personal matter between you and your Lord, we do want to make you aware that our budget goals require that giving levels increase approximately 10 percent. Please participate with us in the gift of giving and of fulfilling our stewardship responsibility as a congregation.

- Second, we request that you fill out the enclosed Estimate of Giving card and place it in the confidential envelope provided.

- Third, please take this card to church on Sunday morning [date], and place it in the special offering. You may also mail this card to the church office if that is more convenient. Either way, rest assured that confidentiality will be strictly maintained by your deacons.

Your estimate of giving is exactly that—an estimate. Your financial situation may change in 1995, enabling you to give less or possibly more to the ministry of this church. However, because stewardship relates to our very identity as Christians, the challenge to plan our giving remains an important one. Because all believers are called to be God's stewards, council's goal during Stewardship Week is to encourage every member to participate meaningfully. Therefore, council members will be contacting those whose cards are not returned. Please return yours promptly.

Council expresses its thanks in advance for your prayerful estimate of financial support. God is doing great things in our congregation. To God be the glory as we enter the new year together.

For the council,
[President of Council]
[Clerk of Council]

ESTIMATE OF GIVING CARD

1996 ESTIMATE OF GIVING CARD

For ministries of Cottonwood Heights
Christian Reformed Church

I/We have prayerfully considered what my/our firstfruit giving should be in [year]. With the help of the Lord, I/we will do my/our best to give for the general fund and building fund as follows:

[ ]_____ weekly OR [ ]_____ monthly

NOTE: Gifts will be automatically allocated to the general and building funds unless otherwise marked below:

$_____ weekly general fund

$_____ weekly building fund

"Each of you must give as you have made up your mind, not reluctantly or under compulsion, for God loves a cheerful giver" (2 Cor. 9:7, NRSV).

FOLLOW-UP STEWARDSHIP CALLS BY COUNCIL MEMBERS

On behalf of the stewardship committee thank you for your willingness to be involved in this concluding chapter of our Stewardship Week. A few general suggestions will help to guide you as you make your calls:

1. It is important to remember that these calls are coming as an official contact from council. Avoid discussing your personal opinions about this program over the phone.

2. Don't argue, make aggressive responses, or consider these calls to be disciplinary. However, you need not be passive or agree with negative statements about what we are doing either. If people misunderstand the program, explain what we are doing and why.

POSSIBLE GREETINGS

Hi [person's first name], I'm [your name] calling for the [church name] council. We have not yet received your [year] estimate-of-giving card, and I am contacting you to encourage you to return the card as soon as possible.

POSSIBLE RESPONSES

Here are some objections and possible responses you may encounter.

Objection: I don't want anyone to know my giving pattern. It's between me and the Lord.

Response: We agree. Your giving should remain confidential. This new system retains the same level of confidentiality as the old system.

Objection: Why do we need this new approach? There's nothing wrong with the one we have now.

Response: Council feels that we should do a better job of financial planning than we have in the past. In order to do that we need a better idea of what the congregation will contribute to the work of the church.

Objection: I misplaced the card I received in the mail.

Response: We have extra cards and confidential envelopes on the counter just inside the church office. Would you be willing to go there tonight and fill out a card and put it in the specially marked stewardship box? Or can we send someone to bring you a card and pick up your estimate of giving?

Objection: Other kingdom causes are also pressing and important. I don't want to commit for a full year.

Response: We're sure you realize that council also has a tough job trying to plan for the programs of a full year of ministry. Your help in this task makes their job a little easier.

Objection: I'm gone much of the year. How can I commit to a weekly or monthly amount?

Response: Just give a yearly total in lieu of a weekly estimate. That will still allow the deacons to plan ahead for next year.

Objection: We just got married, and we're unsure where our church home is going to be.

Response: You can put down a weekly total for as long as your membership continues with us. Just note on the estimate of giving that you're considering a transfer.

Objection: I forgot.

Response: I can sure understand that. It's a busy season. The church will be open this evening. Could you bring it in and place it in the stewardship box in the church office, or can we have someone pick it up?

Objection: I'm in seasonal work. I'm not sure I would be able to fulfill my estimate.

Response: It would be helpful if you just put down a rough estimate for the whole year. That would help council finalize the budget.

Objection: I'm not in the habit of giving in any organized way. I use the loose collection to give as I'm able.

Response: The budget is really a way of planning our giving. It also lets us plan our congregational expenses for all the ministries of our church. Could you give some thought to what your estimate of giving could be for this year? We're only asking for an estimate. We realize that your financial situation may change during the course of the year.

Objection: No. We're not going to hand in the card.

Response: I'm sorry to hear that. We really do need your help in order to do a good job of planning our church budget for the next year. Won't you reconsider? Maybe it would help to talk about this some more. Can we set something up?

CLOSING

Close by thanking them for their time. If they indicate a willingness to fill out a card, be sure to thank them for their participation.

AN EXAMPLE OF A GRADUATED TITHE

Annual Gross Income	%	/Week	/Month
Less than 1,000	4.4	.40	1.80
1,000 - 2,999	4.6	1.80	7.70
3,000 - 4,999	4.8	3.70	16.00
5,000 - 9,999	5.0	7.20	31.00
10,000 - 14,999	5.2	12.50	54.20
15,000 - 19,999	5.4	18.20	78.70
20,000 - 24,999	5.6	24.20	105.00
25,000 - 29,999	5.8	30.37	132.90
30,000 - 39,999	6.0	40.40	175.00
40,000 - 49,999	6.2	59.60	258.30
50,000 - 59,999	6.4	73.80	320.00
60,000 - 69,999	6.6	88.85	385.00
Over 70,000	6.8		

TIMETABLE FOR DEVELOPING A CHURCH BUDGET

August: The treasurer distributes to each committee a report on committee expenditures year-to-date. Committees meet to review expenditures in light of the present budget. Committees craft goals for the next year in their area of ministry and draft a budget that supports the pursuit of these goals.

September: The executive and finance committees meet jointly to review goals and expenses. They take the many pieces of the puzzle and fit them to properly serve the congregation and its vision. They set goals for next year and prepare a tentative church budget proposal.

October, week 1: Council meets to approve the tentative budget and sets a financial goal for the stewardship campaign.

October, week 2: Council sends a letter to all members summarizing the ministry and financial goals for the upcoming year.

October, week 3: Stewardship Week begins in Sunday morning worship with a sermon emphasizing stewardship.

October, week 4: Preaching continues to emphasize stewardship. Members place their estimate-of-giving cards in the offering during the morning service.

November, week 1: Council members place follow-up calls to those who have not turned in a pledge card.

November, week 2: The finance committee adjusts the tentative budget in light of the total estimate of giving for the next year. It consults with the executive committee if the budget requires changes that significantly affect the church's goals.

November, week 3: Council approves the finalized budget.

November, week 4: Council distributes the budget to the congregation for its approval.

December: Council schedules a congregational meeting to approve next year's budget.

BIBLIOGRAPHY

Ballen, S. *Money*. April 1987.

Barrett, Wayne C. *More Money, New Money, Big Money*. Nashville, TN: Discipleship Resources, 1992.

Bassler, Jouette M. *God and Mammon*. Nashville: Abingdon, 1991.

Blue, Ron. *The Debt Squeeze*. Colorado Springs: Focus on the Family, 1989.

_____. *Master Your Money*. Nashville: Nelson, 1991.

Brink, Emily, ed. *Songs for LiFE*. Grand Rapids, MI: CRC Publications, 1994.

Brown, Colin, ed. *The New International Dictionary of New Testament Theology*. Grand Rapids, MI: Zondervan, 1976.

Bruner, Frederick Dale. *Matthew, a Commentary*, Vol. 2. Dallas: Word, 1990.

Callahan, Kennon L. *Twelve Keys to an Effective Church*. San Francisco: Harper and Row, 1983.

_____. *Twelve Keys to an Effective Church: The Leader's Guide*. San Francisco: Harper and Row, 1987.

_____. *Effective Church Leadership: Building on the Twelve Keys*. San Francisco: Harper and Row, 1990.

_____. *Giving and Stewardship in an Effective Church*. San Francisco: Harper and Row, 1992.

_____. *Effective Church Finances*. San Francisco: Harper and Row, 1992.

De Vos, Karen. *Stewardship*. Grand Rapids: CRC Publications, 1987.

Foster, Richard J. *Freedom of Simplicity*. San Francisco: Harper and Row, 1981.

_____. *The Challenge of the Disciplined Life*. San Francisco: Harper Collins, 1985.

Getz, Gene A. *A Biblical Theology of Material Possessions*. Chicago: Moody, 1990.

_____. *Real Prosperity*. Chicago: Moody, 1990.

Gonzalez, Justo L. *Faith and Wealth*. San Francisco: Harper and Row, 1990.

Grimm, Eugene. *Generous People*. Nashville: Abingdon, 1992.

Grissen, Lillian V. *Firstfruits*. Orland Park, IL: Barnabas Foundation, 1992.

Hall, Douglas John. *The Steward: A Biblical Symbol Come of Age*. Grand Rapids: Eerdmans, 1989.

Henry, Carl F. H. *God, Revelation, and Authority*. Waco: Word, 1976.

Hoge, Dean and Douglas Griffin. *Research on Factors Influencing Giving to Religious Bodies*. Indianapolis: Ecumenical Center for Stewardship Studies, 1992.

Kantonen, T. A. *A Theology of Christian Stewardship*. Philadelphia: Muhlenberg, 1956.

McHarg, Ian. *Design with Nature*. Garden City: Natural History Press, 1969.

Myers, David. *The Pursuit of Happiness*. New York: William Morrow, 1992.

Nickle, Keith. *The Collection*. London: SCM, 1966.

Olford, Stephen. *The Grace of Giving*. Grand Rapids: Zondervan, 1972.

Presbyterian Hymnal. Louisville: Westminster/John Knox, 1990.

Reuman, John. *Stewardship and the Economy of God*. Grand Rapids: Eerdmans, 1992.

Robinson, Haddon. "Preaching on Money: When You've Gone Meddlin'," *Preaching*, Vol. 6, March/April 1991, pp. 2-4; 6-10.

Salstrand, George A. E. *The Story of Stewardship in the United States of America*. Grand Rapids: Baker, 1956.

Schneider, John. *Godly Materialism*. Downers Grove: InterVarsity, 1994.

Smit, J. William. *Christian Reformed Charity: A Study of Behavior and Attitudes*. Grand Rapids: Social Research Center, 1979.

Smith, J. W. *The World's Wasted Wealth*. Cambria: Institute for Economic Democracy.

Stott, John. *Decisive Issues Facing Christians Today*. Old Tappan: Fleming H. Revell, 1990.

Stough, Furman C. *Jesus, Dollars and Sense*. New York: Seabury, 1976.

Thompson, T. K., ed. *Stewardship in Contemporary Theology*. New York: Association, 1960.

_____. *Stewardship in Contemporary Life*. New York: Association, 1965.

Van Dyk, Wilbert M. *The Unfinished Story of Stewardship*. Grand Rapids: Calvin Theological Seminary.

von Rad, Gerard. *Genesis: A Commentary, The Old Testament Library*. Philadelphia: Westminster, 1972.

Voogt, Virgil. *Treasure in Heaven*. Ann Arbor: Servant, 1982.

Wilkinson, Loren, ed. *Earthkeeping: Christian Stewardship of Natural Resources*. Grand Rapids: Eerdmans, 1980.

Wuthnow, Robert. *God and Mammon in America*. New York: Free Press, 1994.